What a Character!

HEROES OF THE WAR FOR INDEPENDENCE

Notable Lives from History

Marilyn Boyer

First printing: April 2024
Second printing: April 2025

Master Books, P.O. Box 726, Green Forest, AR 72638

Master Books® is a division of the New Leaf Publishing Group, LLC.

ISBN: 978-1-68344-364-3
ISBN: 978-1-61458-879-5 (digital)
Library of Congress Control Number: 2024933989

Cover: Diana Bogardus
Interior: Terry White

Please consider requesting that a copy of this volume be purchased by your local library system.

Printed in the United States of America

Please visit our website for other great titles:
www.masterbooks.com

For information regarding promotional opportunities,
please contact the publicity department at pr@nlpg.com.

Table of Contents

The War of Independence 5

1. Paul Revere — Rider for Liberty 7
2. John Peter Gabriel Muhlenberg — The Fighting Parson 19
3. Betsy Ross — America's Flag 29
4. John Stark — Hero of Bennington 41
5. Mad Anthony Wayne — The Midnight Attack 51
6. John Sevier — The Battle of Kings Mountain 61
7. Reverend James Caldwell — The Fighting Chaplain 73
8. Nathanael Greene — The Fighting Quaker 83
9. Emily Geiger — A Dangerous Ride 95
10. Marquis de Lafayette — America's Friend 105

Glossary 121

Corresponding Curriculum 125

Endnotes 127

Image Credits

Images are AI-generated at shutterstock.com

Maps:

Map Trek: Atlas of the World & U.S. History – page 6

The War of Independence

The French and Indian War had been fought in the colonies. (Native peoples or Native Americans are terms used more often now.) The British were fighting the French in North America. King George III had his eye on land in Canada and the Ohio River Valley, but French settlements were already there, and the king of France intended to keep them. War seemed to be the only way to resolve the issue. Most of the Native tribes of the region sided with the French and fought fiercely, but the British forces and their native allies won. King George got what he wanted; however, the war proved very costly for Britain. The expenses he accumulated in winning would have a direct bearing on another war 13 years later.

After the French and Indian War, tensions between Britain and its American colonies began to rise. Even though Britain had won the prior war, the cost of it had hurt their economy deeply. To help pay off these debts, Britain started taxing the colonies more. The colonists didn't like this because they felt they should have more say in the decisions that affected them. This led to protests and disagreements between the colonists and the British government. Eventually, these tensions would explode into the American Revolution, where the colonists fought for their independence from Britain.

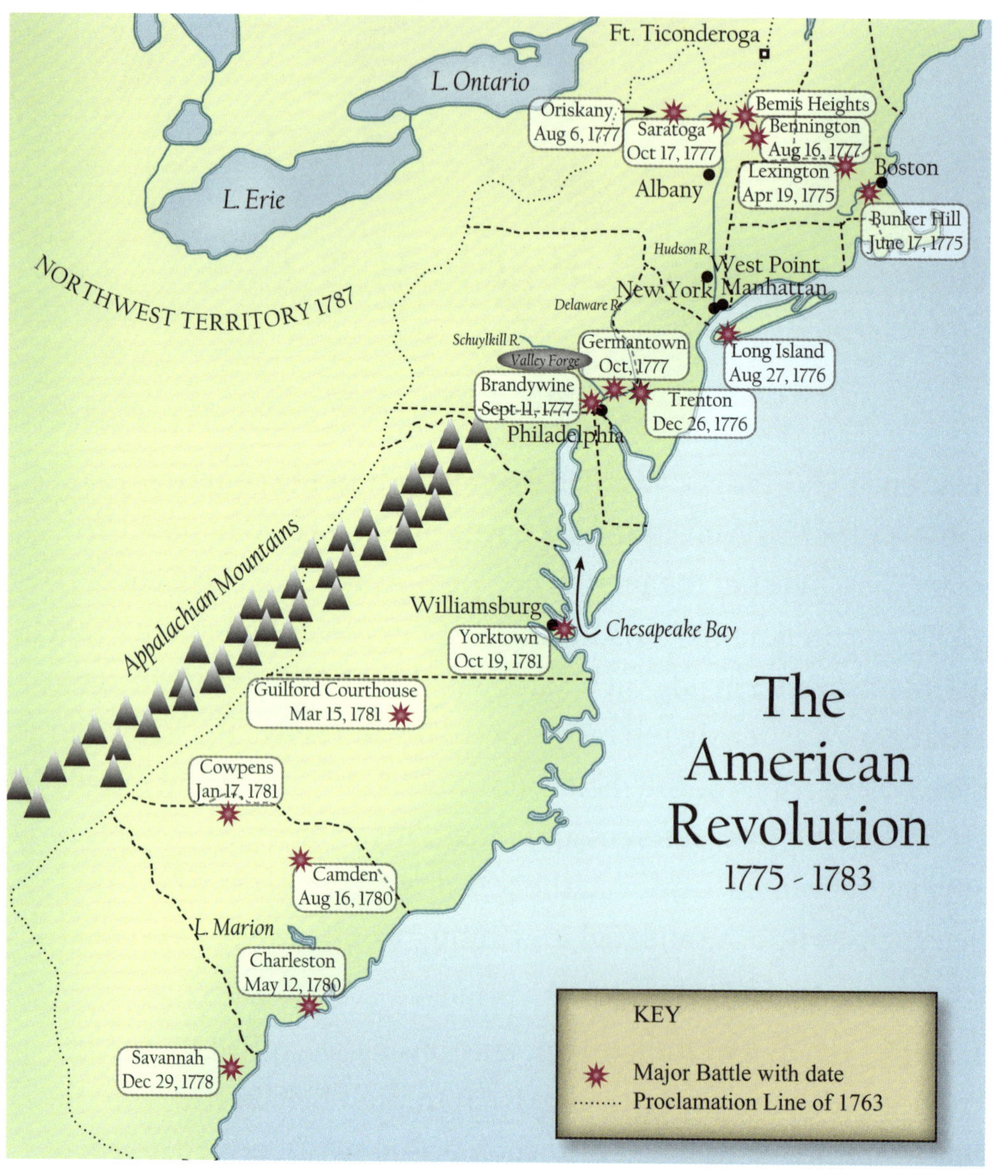

1

Paul Revere – Rider for Liberty

April 18, 1775	Boston, Massachusetts

Who Was Paul Revere?

Paul Revere was born in 1734 and grew up on Fish Street in Boston, Massachusetts. His father **apprenticed** him in the trade of silversmith when he was 13 years old. A silversmith makes things from silver, such as teapots, buttons, buckles, or bracelets. In addition to learning his trade, when Paul was 15, he and some friends were hired to ring the bells in the Old North Church. They learned to play songs by pulling ropes attached to the bells in the church tower. Bell ringing was used to notify the people of Boston that something important was about to happen. In a way, alerting people about crises, although it would take on different forms, became a life-long job for Paul Revere.

apprenticed: Trained

Paul Goes to War

In 1756, Paul, though an American colonist, was still a British citizen. When Britain went to war with the French over disputed territories, Paul joined the British army and went off to fight in the French and Indian War, or so he thought. He was made a lieutenant but never took part in actual fighting. Paul and his troops were sent to **Fort William Henry**, waiting for British generals to give them orders. When the generals finally did arrive, they impressed Paul with how well the troops drilled, thumping their feet down at the same instant. However,

Fort William Henry: A fort near Lake George in New York

the colonists knew that wouldn't work too well when it came to hiding in the woods from the Native peoples.

The British generals wouldn't listen to suggestions from the colonial officers. They looked down on the colonials as inferiors, disregarding the advice they gave. When they did go to battle, the result was devastating. **British General Braddock** was shot down, as were many of the experienced British officers. If it hadn't been for a young officer from Virginia named George Washington, they might all have been killed, but Washington knew how to fight the Native peoples. Paul Revere hadn't been involved in the battle, and his unit was sent home after almost a year of inactivity. He returned a bit disgusted with the British generals who had no use for the colonists and insisted on doing things their way even when common sense should have told them otherwise.

British General Braddock: Commander in chief for the 13 colonies

Back to Boston

Paul resumed working as a silversmith and expanded his skills. He learned to make false teeth, and he taught himself **engraving**. Soon after Paul came back to Boston, he married 21-year-old Sarah Orne, a girl he met at church. They would eventually have eight children. Paul was a good father. Once, when one of

engraving: Cutting designs in silver to print on paper

his children came down with the dreaded and often deadly disease of smallpox, he insisted on caring for the child at home instead of carrying him off to the **pest house**, as was commonly done.

The whole family had to be **quarantined** for a full month, but he stuck by his decision. The entire family came safely through the sickness. He had to work extra hard to make up for having his business shut down for a whole month. Fortunately, his business began to flourish, and Paul did well, making beautifully detailed creamers, bowls, cups, silverware, and whatever people needed. Today, some of the pieces Paul made are on display in some of America's finest museums.

pest house: House where sick people stayed until they got well or died

quarantined: Kept at home to prevent the spread of germs

Unrest Brewing

Great Britain began taxing the colonists. The British government had many debts, some of which had accumulated during the French and Indian War. **Parliament** decided the colonists must help pay the bills. The colonists didn't mind paying their share, but resented the government instituting and enforcing taxes without their **consent**. Besides, King George had really waged the war to acquire more land, not to benefit the colonists.

Parliament: British ruling body

consent: Permission

The only fair kind of government is based on law, not the whim of a king or his Parliament. The new taxes were just the beginning of a long list of **usurpations** by King George. Patriotic colonists started to meet in The Green Dragon in Boston's North End to decide how to handle the troubling situation. They called themselves the Sons of Liberty. Paul was one of the leaders of the group. The meetings were secret; the members started wearing a special medal around their neck to identify themselves to one another. Paul made the medals, which bore an image of the Liberty Tree. The Liberty Tree was a large elm tree that stood on the **Boston Common** and was then nearly 120 years old. The Sons of Liberty would meet there and sometimes have peaceful protests against British **tyranny**.

usurpations: Abuses of power to control others

Boston Common: Historic public park located in downtown Boston

tyranny: Cruel, Oppressive rule

implemented: Put in place

In March 1765, Parliament had **implemented** the Stamp Act, which placed a tax on documents, newspapers, marriage licenses, almanacs, and other papers. Unable to collect the taxes, Britain repealed the tax a year later. The colonists were elated and thought this meant they would be treated fairly. That night, they decorated the Liberty Tree and celebrated around it.

More Taxes

However, in 1767, Parliament passed the Townshend Acts, which **imposed** taxes on glass, lead, paint, paper, and tea. The colonists **appealed** many times to King George but to no avail. They wanted to elect colonists to go to England to represent them in Parliament, as is the right of British citizens. The Massachusetts legislature sent a letter to other state legislatures encouraging them to oppose the unfair taxes. King George was furious when he found out and sent an army to occupy the city of Boston. British soldiers stayed in the houses of Boston residents without permission and often demanded free food.

imposed: Forced

appealed: Made an earnest plea

Due to protests from the colonists, as well as from some of the members of Parliament, the Townshend Acts were removed in 1770, except for the tax on tea. Parliament thought the colonists wouldn't make a fuss over this tax on their favorite drink. They were wrong. The colonists agreed together to stop drinking tea. They would make do without it. About this time, according to the records of the Revere family, Paul acquired a horse. He built a stable to house the animal. His neighbors soon found out why he needed that horse: he became a crucial **courier** for the Sons of Liberty, delivering messages throughout the colonies, a responsibility which placed his life in constant danger.

courier: Messenger

The Boston Tea Party

The Sons of Liberty decided to show Parliament and King George that they would not submit to unlawful taxes. On the night of December 16, 1773, a group of Patriots dressed up as Native people, smeared their faces with soot and red paint, and rowed out to the three British cargo ships in the harbor. The ships had just arrived with a new shipment of tea. If no one bought the tea, then no taxes could be collected on it. They used axes to chop holes in 342 tea chests and dumped over 90,000 pounds of tea into Boston Harbor. Paul Revere was one of those Patriots and gave himself the name of "Mohawk." The Sons of Liberty did not hurt anyone or destroy any part of the ship, but they made it obvious they would not pay tax on that tea. The event became known as the Boston Tea Party.

King George was furious when he found out and demanded that the people of Boston pay for the tea they dumped in the water. He ordered Boston Harbor to be closed — no boats or ships could enter or leave. Many Bostonians relied on **commerce** to earn money for food, clothes, and necessities. Ships were an essential means of transporting those

commerce: Buying and selling goods

goods. What could be done? Paul saddled his horse and rode off to carry the message of Boston's **plight** to the other colonies. This journey became the first of many important rides for Paul Revere. As the news reached the other colonies, supplies began coming in. The rest of the Americans would stand with Boston and keep them supplied with food and necessary items while the harbor remained closed off.

During this time, Paul Revere began watching the British more closely. He had to be very cautious. He knew he could be arrested for spying, and spies were usually hung. He wrote, "In the winter, towards spring, we frequently took turns, two and two, to watch the soldiers, by patrolling the streets all night."[1] By mid-April the colonists were **stockpiling** ammunition to prepare for what they felt would be an unavoidable war. General Thomas Gage was leading the British army at the time. He decided to **confiscate** all of the colonists' guns in Charlestown, right across the river from Boston. Paul overheard that Gage also planned a march to Fort William and Mary in New Hampshire to confiscate colonists' guns. That's where Paul's newly acquired horse came in again! Paul rode all night to warn the colonists in New Hampshire to hide all their guns and ammunition.

plight: Difficult situation

stockpiling: Storing up

confiscate: Seize

Riding for Liberty

There was a large store of guns in the town of Concord, Massachusetts, which lay 12 miles from Boston. The Patriots found out that this was Gage's next target. He had placed **sentries** on all the roads between neighboring towns. Gage also had orders to arrest John Hancock and Samuel Adams, and send them to England for trial as **traitors**. Paul and the Sons of Liberty had devised a plan to warn colonists about the movement of British troops. What they needed to know was whether the **Redcoats** would move out "by water" across the Charles River to Cambridge or begin marching "by land" from Boston Neck.

sentries: Soldier guards

traitors: Betrayers of one's country

Redcoats: Nickname for British soldiers because of their red uniforms

sexton: Person who looks after a church

Robert Newman, the **sexton** of the Old North Church, had been chosen to give the signal from the church steeple tower. He was to hang two lanterns if the British were leaving by boat. If they started marching by land, he was to hang only one lantern. This signal would alert Patriots on the Charlestown shore which way the British were coming in case the messenger himself could not make it there from Boston to start his ride.

It was April 18, 1785, when Paul Revere heard from several reliable sources what was to happen. He hurried over to tell Robert Newman to hang two lanterns and then hurried home to gather his gear and bid his family goodbye. He charged his son to care for the family if anything should happen to him. They all knew his mission was **perilous**. He tried to encourage his son: "And as for being hanged, we all have to die, son,

perilous: Very dangerous

sometime. You can't dodge that. The important thing is to be ready to die bravely, whether you stop a bullet when you're young, or die in your bed of old age …"[2]

Paul swiftly headed to where he'd hidden his rowboat. He had to cross the Charles River, so was not able to take his own horse. His plan was to quietly row across the river, hopefully escaping notice of the British warship *Somerset*, anchored in the harbor. Arriving at his boat, he realized he'd forgotten his spurs, which he needed to be able to get a horse to move fast. His dog had followed him to the river. Writing a note to his wife, he attached it to his dog's collar. "Home boy, home as fast as you can," he said. The dog was off like a shot and back in a few minutes with his spurs tied to his neck.

Paul did manage to sneak past the British and cross the river. On the other side, he met some men who led him to Deacon Larkin's house. The deacon loaned Paul a swift horse named Brown Beauty. He mounted and headed swiftly toward Lexington, waking the sleeping villagers as he cried out, "Up and arm, the regulars are coming!"[3] These regulars were the British army.

Minutemen soon heard the alarm — the sounds of guns and the excited ringing of church bells. The countrymen were rising and preparing to defend their homes. At Lexington, Minutemen guarding the house where Sam Adams and John Hancock were sleeping ordered Revere not to make so much noise. "You will soon have noise enough. The regulars are coming!" he shouted.[4] Revere was captured by British sentries on his way to Concord. Amazingly, the soldiers let him go, but kept Brown Beauty. Thankfully, at least two other riders that night didn't get caught: William Dawes and Wentworth Cheswell. The word was spreading far and wide, and when the British arrived at Lexington, John Hancock and Sam Adams had made their escape, and the Minutemen were armed and waiting for the British. It was the beginning of the American War of Independence.

Minutemen: Colonists ready to fight at a minute's notice

Revere continued to risk his life for the rest of the war. He learned to make gunpowder and kept American forces supplied with ammunition. He also made the engravings for **Continental money**. He made many rides to warn and inform others of what was happening. He is, though, most famous

Continental money: Paper money issued by the Continental Congress during the war

for that brave ride on April 18, 1775, forever remembered in a poem by Henry Wadsworth Longfellow entitled "Paul Revere's Ride."

Paul Revere died when he was 83. He had more than 50 grandchildren, whom he dearly loved. Today, near the Old North Church in Boston, a statue of Paul Revere, on his horse in mid-gallop, stands to commemorate his ride at the start of the war that birthed America.

2

John Peter Gabriel Muhlenberg— The Fighting Parson

1776–1783	Woodstock, Virginia, Charleston, Brandywine, Stony Point, and Yorktown

During the American War of Independence, preachers played a vital role. They addressed current issues in sermons, teaching their people to think biblically. Sam Adams, who is known as the "Father of the American Revolution," said it was actually Reverend Jonathan Mayhew of the West Congregational Church in Boston who deserved that title. John Adams called Mayhew, "the morning gun of the revolution." Mayhew preached several sermons on Romans 13. These were printed and distributed throughout the colonies. A copy was even sent to King George, challenging him to repent of his tyrannies. His sermon resulted in the **motto**, "Resistance to tyrants is obedience to God."

motto: Rallying cry

King George mocked the preachers of the Revolution, calling them "The Black Robed Regiment," because of the robes they wore during services. Captured members of the "Black Robe Regiment" were treated especially brutally by the British. The colonists looked to Scripture for answers to everyday life. Much of the Declaration of Independence and the Constitution reflects their practical knowledge of the Scriptures. Events happening around them had to be seen in light of the Word of God. The preachers understood that their job was to instruct the people to be skillful with the Scriptures.

Who Was John Peter Gabriel Muhlenberg?

John Peter Gabriel Muhlenberg was born on October 1, 1746, the son of a Lutheran minister who had immigrated to this country four years earlier. His parents named him after the three pastors who served as the infant's godparents at his baptism: John Kurtz, Peter Brunnholtz, and Gabriel Naesmann. For most of his life, he was known as Peter. He learned to speak both English and German. As a boy, he loved to hunt and fish in the woods around his home in Trappe, Pennsylvania. He was educated first in the colonies and then briefly in Europe. He was made a minister in 1768 at age 22 and began preaching. He assisted his father in the pulpit and filled in at various churches in southeastern Pennsylvania that didn't have regular pastors. His ability to speak two languages was beneficial to the congregations.

Peter married Anna Meyer in 1770. Soon after their marriage, he accepted a call to a pulpit in Woodstock, Virginia. There were many German settlers in the Shenandoah Valley region. He ministered in two churches — one English and one German. He answered the call because he believed his training equipped him for this ministry. The community grew to love Muhlenberg. He was elected to the Virginia House of Burgesses. As a result he was present at St. John's Church in Richmond, when Patrick Henry gave his famous, inspirational speech, "Give me liberty or give me death."

Raising of Arms

In January 1776, the Virginia Convention voted to raise arms and equip militiamen. War had already begun in Massachusetts. Virginians needed to be prepared, as it was **inevitable** that the conflict would reach them soon. The German men of the Shenandoah Valley region made up the majority of the Eighth Battalion. They chose Pastor Muhlenberg to be their colonel. His appointment pleased both George Washington and Patrick Henry. They knew soldiers would follow a strong, dedicated leader. They were concerned that because the British hired **Hessian mercenaries**, the German farmers might support the British cause. With Muhlenberg at the **helm**, they would have a solid, dependable leader to inspire men to fight for their liberties.

inevitable: Sure to happen

Farewell Sermon

Muhlenberg returned to Woodstock to **recruit** men, and then organize, equip, and drill them. His congregation flocked to church upon his return, realizing that this might be the last sermon he would preach. The church was jam-packed — actually overflowing. People were standing on the burial ground that

Hessian mercenaries: German soldiers paid to fight

helm: Head

recruit: Sign up for the army

surrounded the church, straining to hear. Muhlenberg's farewell sermon "glowed throughout with the most devoted patriotism. At the close, he told them of the resolution he had taken to fight, and if need be, die for his country on the battlefield."[5] Dressed in his black minister's robe, he ended his sermon by saying, "The Bible tells us there is a time to preach, and a time to pray, but the time for me to preach has passed away."[6] Then raising his voice till it rung like the blast of a trumpet he exclaimed, "There is a time to pray and a time to fight, and that time has now come."[7]

After pronouncing the **benediction**, he removed his black robe and stood before his astonished congregation in the uniform of a Virginia colonel. Only after removing his robe, did he place his sword at his side. One account says the congregation burst into singing, "A Mighty Fortress Is Our God." The sight of a Virginia colonel walking down the aisle in place of their pastor took everyone by surprise! He promptly strode to the door and ordered the drum to beat for recruits. The spell-bound congregation suddenly rose to their feet.

benediction: Blessing at the end of a service

All the men able to **bear arms** began to flock around their former pastor. The calm, quiet Sabbath day was transformed into a whirlwind of excitement. The drum kept beating. Men who had not been in the church for the sermon came rushing over to see what was going on. The sight of the former pastor in uniform as he called for recruits kindled much enthusiasm, and soon 300 men had joined his brigade.

bear arms: Carry guns

Off to Battle

The Eighth Battalion immediately began to march south. A month later, on July 23, 1776, they reached Charleston — just in time for the battle. The British warships began their bombardment of Sullivan's Island on the 28th. They tried to land their troops, but Muhlenberg's regiment sprang into action and repelled the attack. The British were driven back to their ships. General Lee was astonished by the bravery of the Virginians and reported, "I know not which corps I have the greatest reason to be pleased with, Muhlenberg's Virginians or the North Carolina troops; they were both equally alert, zealous, and spirited."[8]

The following year, Muhlenberg was promoted to Brigadier General and took charge of all the Continental troops in Virginia. He made the wise suggestion to Washington that the men be equipped with **muskets** instead of rifles, explaining that they were exposed to bad weather quite often. Muskets were not as affected by the weather as rifles. His first assignment was to recruit more men and send them to Washington's army in northern New Jersey. He joined General Washington in May 1777 and spent the next winter and spring in the **desolate** camp at Valley Forge, suffering **deprivation** together with all his men. Muhlenberg supported his

muskets: Light guns with a long barrel

desolate: Bleak

deprivation: Lack of basic necessities

commander in chief with devotion. His commitment gave hope to his men through the trials of that terrible winter.

Brandywine, Germantown, Monmouth, Stony Point

At Brandywine, Muhlenberg's brigade was one of the divisions under General Nathanael Greene. At the close of that disastrous day, Muhlenberg was ordered up from the rear to cover the **retreat**. For three-quarters of an hour, his courageous troops held back the entire British army, allowing Greene's men to retreat in safety before they withdrew as well. At Germantown, General Muhlenberg was in the thickest part of the battle. Some of his regiments had to engage in **bayonet** fighting.

retreat: Withdraw

bayonet: Blades on muskets

Muhlenberg's horse was almost totally exhausted from jumping fences. Some of his men had to help by pulling down fences to spare his horse. There were several instances when British sharpshooters made Muhlenberg their specific target, and bullets whizzed around him. Once he saw a British officer raise his gun to fire at him, but Muhlenberg was quicker and shot the officer first.

Greene was forced to order a retreat because the British were being reinforced, and the Americans were in danger of being trapped along the Germantown road. Muhlenberg's troops again covered the retreat of Greene's men and, as at Brandywine, were last to leave. At Monmouth, on a blistering hot Sabbath day, General Muhlenberg led troops over the steaming sands without wavering. Due to Muhlenberg's coolness, courage, and **determination**, General Anthony Wayne selected him to command the reserve troops at the attack of Stony Point.

Yorktown

Muhlenberg took an active role in the siege of Yorktown. He helped devise the trap set for Cornwallis and his men that led to the end of the war. On one occasion, he led troops to storm a **redoubt**, and due to his determination and skill, he accomplished the mission without losing any of his men. Before the arrival of Washington at Yorktown, Lafayette feared that Cornwallis would attempt to break through the American lines to escape to North Carolina. The task of keeping him at Yorktown was assigned to Anthony Wayne's and Peter Muhlenberg's men.

determination: Strong decision to accomplish a goal

redoubt: Temporary fortification

Muhlenberg ordered the North Carolina militia to destroy bridges, mills, and provisions. Then he posted troops close to the British line at Yorktown to keep watch on their movements.

On September 27, Washington placed the brigades of Muhlenberg and Hazen on the right of the front line under the command of Lafayette. On the night of October 15, two brigades of Americans under Muhlenberg captured one of the two British redoubts. Muhlenberg was slightly injured in this mission.

The report of this storming of the redoubt read, Muhlenberg "displayed the hero, the human man and gave a luster to the name of American by blending valor and intrepidity ... having entered the breach and every man of his party, including himself, wounded, he stayed the hand of his fellow citizens from the exercise of the lawful rights of war; he stormed, conquered, and spared the vanquished."[9] Muhlenberg was praised for giving mercy to the captured enemy. Shortly after this, he came down with a violent fever and requested permission to go home until he recovered. He remained with his family until the following spring.

After the War

On September 30, 1783, Congress promoted General Muhlenberg to the rank of Major General. The war was over, and the army disbanded the following November. On returning to Woodstock, his congregation begged him to resume the ministry. His answer was, "It would never do to mount the parson after the soldier."[10] His Woodstock church from which he had preached his thrilling farewell sermon dispersed after the war.

Peter Muhlenberg moved his family from Woodstock, Virginia, back to his parents' home in Trappe, Pennsylvania. He was appointed chairman of the executive council of the state and afterward sent to Congress. In 1801, Peter Muhlenberg was elected to the United States Senate. That year he also was appointed as Supervisor of the Internal Revenue of Pennsylvania. In 1802, he became Collector of the Port of Philadelphia and held that position until his death in October 1807. Muhlenberg was buried near the church where he was baptized. Above his grave is the inscription: "He was brave in the field, faithful in the cabinet, honorable in all transactions, a sincere friend, and an honest man."[11]

A person may wonder why John Peter Gabriel Muhlenberg left the pulpit for the army. This is how he defended his decision in a letter to his brother, who was also a pastor: "Do you think if America should be conquered, I should be safe? Far from it. And would you not sooner fight like a man than die like a dog? I am called by my country to its defence (an old spelling of defense). The cause is just and noble. Were I a bishop, even a Lutheran one, I should obey without hesitation, and so far am I from thinking I am wrong, I am convinced it is my duty to do so, a duty I owe to my God and to my country."[12]

3

Betsy Ross – America's Flag

1775–1783	Philadelphia, Pennsylvania

The American War of Independence was fought between 1775 and 1783. The colonists believed they were not being given the rights of British citizens or even a say in how they were governed. The actual war began with the Battle of Lexington and Concord on April 19, 1775. Shortly after, the colonies formed the Continental Congress to deal with the situation. George Washington was appointed commander in chief of the Continental Army. The colonists who believed America should be free from British rule were called Patriots. Betsy Ross was one of those Patriots.

Who was Betsy Ross?

Elizabeth (better known as Betsy) Griscom was born on January 1, 1752, on a farm in West Jersey, the 9th of 17 children born to Samuel and Rebecca Griscom. Two years later her family moved to Philadelphia, the largest city in the American colonies.

The Griscoms were Quakers, deeply religious people who believed it was wrong to bear arms. They lived very plain, simple lives but enjoyed picnics, skating, and sledding.

Betsy finished her schooling at age 12. Great Aunt Sarah, her father's aunt, lived with the Griscoms. She and Betsy did most of the sewing and mending

for the family. Aunt Sarah had started her own sewing business as a young woman. She and Betsy had always shared a special friendship, likely because they were both gifted at needlework and shared the quality of determination.

About this time, Betsy's father decided it was time for Betsy to learn a trade. He settled on the **upholstery** business, and a Quaker friend, John Webster, took her on as an apprentice. An apprentice was not paid but is given the opportunity to learn a skill by doing it. Betsy's apprenticeship included many more skills than just upholstery, such as making **draperies**, tablecloths, flags, carpets, blankets, tents, and more. Betsy took pride in her work. Each evening she and Great Aunt Sarah loved to share about what she had worked on during the day. Betsy had learned so much over the years from Great Aunt Sarah; someday she hoped to have a shop of her own too.

upholstery: Fabric-covered furniture

draperies: Curtains

John Ross

Betsy made many friends while working at Webster's. One of those friends was a young man named John Ross, also an apprentice. She and John discovered they had a lot in common. Both had lost siblings whom they had helped to raise. And both wanted to open their own upholstery shops! Over time, Betsy and John's relationship grew and they desired to be married. There was one big problem though. John was the son of an **Anglican** minister and not a Quaker.

The Quaker religion prevented its members from marrying anyone who was not a Quaker. If Betsy married John, she was sure to be asked to leave the Society of Friends, as the Quakers were called. Their rule read, "Mixing in Marriage with Those not of our Professions is an unequal Yoking which brings ill Consequences to the Parties as well as Grief to their honest Friends and Relatives and frequently ends in Woe and Ruin of Themselves and their Children."[13] John and Betsy, believing it was the right thing to do, decided to marry despite Betsy's dismissal from the Society of Friends. John and Betsy were both 21 years of age. In preparation for providing for his family, John opened an upholstery shop of his own on February 24, 1773. On November 4, 1773, the couple was married and settled into John's home.

Anglican: Church of England

Tea Trouble

As newlyweds, John and Betsy were working hard to build up their business. Trouble, however, was brewing. Philadelphia was in turmoil over Great Britain's tax on tea. Parliament had ruled that American colonies could only buy tea from the British East India Tea Company, and with it came a tax. Parliament did not give the colonies a voice or vote about the tax; it was just imposed. The Continental Congress met for the first time on September 5, 1774, at Carpenter's Hall in Philadelphia, near Betsy and John's shop. The Congress sent letters to King George III demanding the right to "life, liberty, and property." King George ignored them. Many people in America realized that the only way to break away from British rule would be to fight. They began stockpiling ammunition and training to fight. John Ross became a Minuteman.

John and Betsy's business was growing. Betsy saw signs of approaching war, such as all sorts of new flags: Don't Tread on Me, New England's Pine Tree Flag, Rhode Island's white flag with its blue anchor and 13 stars. Swords, pistols, muskets, and **knapsacks** filled the hardware shop. Men volunteered to join the militia and drilled every night after their work. On June 23, 1775, John and Betsy and their neighbors gathered on the street to watch as George Washington's newly formed troops marched out of Philadelphia. Bands played and flags waved in the wind.

knapsacks: Backpacks

DONT TREAD ON ME

British soldiers were not in Philadelphia yet, but Betsy and John knew they were coming. In the meantime, they would continue to work six days a week in their shop. John, as part of the militia, trained each night after work. While waiting for Washington to call them to duty, men in the militia guarded Philadelphia, protecting the gunpowder, cannons, and muskets stored in the town. Betsy would straighten up the shop, tend to the fire, lock up each evening, and often head to bed to wait for John to come home from his duties.

Tragedy Strikes

One night, just before morning, Betsy was awakened by a knock on the door. She reached out to wake John but realized he wasn't there. A group of men stood at the door, bearing a wounded man. It was John! The men explained that John had been making his rounds of stored ammunition and there had been an explosion. John was badly hurt. They carried him to his bed and Betsy called the doctor, cleaned his wounds, fed him broth, and cared for him. Within a few days, however, on January 21, 1776, John died. Betsy was devastated. John was buried in the cemetery of Christ Church, the church the couple attended.

Betsy, now 24 years old, felt all alone, but that night she bravely decided to continue to run the business she and John had worked so hard to build. Having watched Great Aunt Sarah run a business by herself, Betsy thought, "If she could do it, I will too!"

Hard Times

Betsy hung a sign over her shop that read, "Elizabeth Ross, Upholsterer." Business had slowed down due to the impending war. To make ends meet, Betsy began sewing uniforms for the soldiers. Congress was meeting at the State House, and delegates sometimes needed new clothes. Betsy's grandson reported years later that George Washington went to Betsy's shop when he needed new shirts. "While he was yet Colonel, Washington had visited her shop both professionally and socially many times."[14]

John's uncle, George Ross, who would be one of the signers of the Declaration of Independence, was a good friend of George Washington. They all attended Christ Church together. The war actually turned out to help Betsy's business. Soldiers needed blankets and bedding, armies needed tents and

cots, and everyone needed flags. Each unit of the army needed to have its own flag. Ships flew flags and each one had to be made by hand. They not only had to look good, but had to be sturdy enough to stand up against the wind and weather.

A New Flag

In the spring of 1776, the colonies did not have a single flag that represented all of them together. The leaders of the colonies began to think it would be a boost to the men to have one flag the Americans could call their own. George Washington decided to work with Congressman George Ross and Congressman Robert Morris, a wealthy ship owner who raised much money for the Continental Army, to design a national flag. George Ross recommended his nephew's widow, Betsy Ross, who was known to be a skilled seamstress and fine Patriot woman.

It had been more than five months since John died when Betsy answered the door one morning to find three men at her doorstep. She knew them all — Uncle George Ross, Robert Morris, and General George Washington. They didn't waste time inquiring if Betsy thought she could help them out. General Washington showed her a sketch they had created. It was a square flag with thirteen red and white stripes, one stripe representing each colony. A blue square in the upper left corner had six-pointed stars. A circle of stars, they explained, represented the union of the colonies, one star for each state, blue represented a strong color, white a pure color, and red a brave color. They asked if Betsy had any suggestions.

She respectfully suggested that the flag should be rectangular, as were most other flags. She then showed them how a five-pointed star would be faster and easier to make. Washington and the other men were impressed with her suggestions and asked her to start constructing the new flag. They needed it as quickly as possible, because General Washington was leaving Philadelphia soon.

George Ross gave her money to buy fabric and supplies. Robert Morris told her to go to his shipping wharf where one of his clerks would furnish her with the fabric. Betsy chose the **bunting** carefully and purchased some heavier needles than she had used before. Betsy closed her shop for a few days and immediately started on the flag, working well into the night. What Betsy didn't know at the time was that while she was busy sewing America's first flag, Thomas Jefferson was at work writing the Declaration of Independence, just doors away.

bunting: Heavy cloth used to make flags

The Flag Is Finished

As soon as Betsy finished, she contacted George Ross, who came by to pick up the flag. He returned later in the day to report that General Washington had been very pleased with her work. He also told her to make as many flags as she could, as quickly as possible. He said he would bring her money from time to time to continue the work. The colonies needed many flags! On July 4, 1776, Congress voted to approve the Declaration of Independence, and the city celebrated.

Not many months later, Betsy heard of Washington's incredible victory on Christmas night, when his soldiers marched on Trenton and then Princeton a few days later.

Over the winter Betsy became reacquainted with an old friend, Joseph Ashburn. Their relationship deepened and they were married in June 1777. The day before their wedding, the Second Continental Congress passed a resolution that the flag she had made for George Washington a year earlier was now the official flag of the United States.

More Trouble

Soon there were rumors that the British were about to invade Philadelphia. Congress fled to Baltimore, but Betsy stayed, keeping her shop open. At dawn on October 4, 1777, the Battle of Germantown began. Casualties were heavy on both sides, but the British were victorious. Wagons began to arrive, carrying the wounded. Nearly 700

Americans had been badly injured. Families opened their homes to care for the men, and Betsy and many other women hurried to help. The women nursed the wounded, assisted in surgeries, and made bandages. They cooked soups and brought in blankets and clothing from their own homes.

British soldiers, meanwhile, **plundered** household goods, silverware, paintings, jewelry, and food. Because of the British occupation of Philadelphia during the winter of 1777–78, Betsy had no way to keep her house warm. Every morning the water in her bedside basin was frozen. Her hands were so cold it was hard to thread her needles. It was June 1778 when the British finally left the city, and Betsy could return to making flags.

plundered: Robbed

For the next year, Joseph was a privateersman, which is someone who works on a ship authorized for use in war but owned by individuals holding a government commission. He regularly sailed from Philadelphia to the West Indies. Betsy always hated to see him go. Besides running the shop, she worked for the army loading cartridges with powder and musket balls. On September 15, 1779, Betsy gave birth to her first child, Zillah.

Business had grown, and she now hired seamstresses occasionally to help her. Joseph returned home for a brief time but left on another voyage in October 1780. By now, Betsy was expecting again. When she hadn't heard from Joseph by the end of November, she was worried. Voyages normally lasted only six weeks. Baby

Eliza was born on February 15, 1781, and still no sign of Joseph.

The War Is Over

In October 1781, news came that the war was finally over. Although Betsy rejoiced with the rest of the country, she was quite concerned for Joseph. It was August 15 when a childhood friend, John Claypoole, knocked on her door. He had been on the same ship as Joseph. He told her they had been captured by the British and held at Old Mill Prison in Plymouth, England. Joseph had gotten sick in February and died in March. Betsy was a widow for the second time, and now she had two little girls to care for.

John visited Betsy often and told her how Joseph and he had supported each other while in prison. Betsy and John talked of fun times they remembered having together as children. John decided to give up his job at sea and find a job in Philadelphia. He asked Betsy to marry him, and on May 8, 1783, they were married in Christ Church. John helped Betsy with the shop, and the business prospered. Betsy gave birth to her third daughter in 1785.

Betsy continued making flags. The War of 1812 supplied her with many orders from the U.S. Army and Navy. The family grew, and when her daughters and nieces were old enough, Betsy taught them everything she knew, just as Great Aunt Sarah had **mentored** her. Betsy's loving, generous spirit made her everyone's favorite. On January 30, 1836, Betsy passed away when she was 84. In the words of her grandson, "She was beloved and respected by all who had ever known her."[15]

mentored: Trained

The Betsy Ross House is one of the most famous historic sites in Philadelphia today. A flag is flown day and night in honor of Betsy's contributions to the birth of the United States of America.

4

John Stark—Hero of Bennington

August 16, 1777	The War of Independence

Things weren't looking especially good for the Americans. In the summer of 1777, the British army under General John Burgoyne had just succeeded in recapturing Fort Ticonderoga. That was the fort captured by Ethan Allen in the early days of the War of Independence. Although this was a victory for the British, they were running dangerously low on food, ammunition, and necessary supplies. Burgoyne had to find a way to stock up on supplies for his large army — and fast.

Who Was John Stark?

John Stark grew up on a New Hampshire farm. There wasn't a school nearby, so his parents taught him to read and write. John was intelligent and liked to learn. He especially liked accounting and history, but he also became very skilled in working with lumber and wood. By the time he was in his twenties, he was an expert hunter, trapper, and guide through the New Hampshire wilderness. Once, on a hunting trip with his brother and two friends, he was captured by some Native people. They eventually came to respect John's bravery and named him "Young Chief." He was held captive for two months

until officials from Massachusetts bought his freedom. John had learned much about Native American **tactics** during those two months that would prove extremely valuable in years to come.

Rogers' Rangers

During the French and Indian War, Britain formed a company of men known as Rogers' Rangers under the command of Robert Rogers. The Rangers were known for their bravery, skill in the woods, and fierce fighting. Robert Rogers chose John Stark to be the second lieutenant in the outfit. The way Rangers fought was different from other soldiers. One of their main functions was to act as scouts to gather information about the enemy. They wore dull-colored clothing to blend in with the forest. They were to note the condition of the enemy's fort and to estimate the number of soldiers. They would then report their discoveries back to their officers. When the French surrendered in 1760, The French and Indian War came to a close, but John Stark had proven himself a fearless leader of men. Later on, his country would again look to him for leadership.

tactics: Plan of action

Home Again

Eight days before his 31st birthday, John married 21-year-old Elizabeth Page. John loved to call people by nicknames, and he gave Elizabeth the nickname of "Molly." John bought more land, built a home, and became a successful farmer and lumberman. He and Molly had 11 children. They enjoyed a happy life together. John was elected to the New Hampshire Committee of Safety. Upon hearing of the Battle of Lexington and Concord in Massachusetts, he left home immediately, "hastening forward from his sawmill in his shirt sleeves."[16] He rode his horse 70 miles to Cambridge to join the Patriot army.

As he made his way south, he called out to all the men he passed, appealing to them to drop what they were doing, grab their muskets, and join him. He was joined by hundreds of New Hampshire men ready to fight for liberty. John Stark was chosen to be their colonel. He began to train the men to stand still in line, how to march in step, and how to load and fire their muskets together in a **volley**. He worked to get supplies for his poorly equipped men.

volley: Many bullets shot at the same time

The Battle of Bunker Hill*

It had been six weeks since the Battle of Lexington and Concord. The British were occupying Boston. North of Boston, across a half mile of water, lay Charlestown. On the night of June 16, 1775, one thousand New Englanders began to build a redoubt on Breed's Hill to the north of Charlestown. From the top of the hill, the Americans would be in a good position to fire on the British below. Colonel Stark received orders on the following day to take several hundred of his New Hampshire troops to Breed's Hill, where the British were preparing to attack the redoubt.

When they arrived, the cannons on the British warships were targeting anyone who tried to cross Charlestown Neck. Unafraid, Stark led his soldiers forward to fill a gap on the Americans' left **flank**. Many men crammed into the redoubt. To the left, a farm road between two rail fences extended down the hill to the banks of the Mystic River. Connecticut troops lined most of the fence, but beyond them, it was left undefended. Colonel Stark saw that the British could push past the Americans' left side, cutting off their only way of retreat. He had his men cover the rail fence with hay to give it the appearance of being solid. He also had them pile rocks onto the beach to help fill the gap.

flank: Side

*Note: The battle is named after Bunker Hill which was the original objective of both the colonial and British troops, though the majority of combat took place on the adjacent Breed's Hill.

Then he gave his men a short but motivating speech just before the British began to arrive.

The British planned to attack, concentrating near the rail fence and on the beach. From there, they planned to move to Breed's Hill and attack the redoubt from the left flank. What the British neglected to consider was the determination of Stark's men. They were overwhelmed by how fast the Americans fired and reloaded. Forced to fall back, they suffered a terrible loss of men. On the beach in front of Stark's men, a British officer described the dead, saying they "lay as thick as sheep in a fold."[17] By dusk that day, the British had achieved their objective, but only because the Americans ran out of ammunition. The British were victorious, but at a grievous cost. More than 1,000 British soldiers were killed or wounded. The Americans had 450 casualties.

The Battle of Bennington

It was the summer of 1777. British troops led by General John Burgoyne moved south from Canada, hoping to divide New England from the rest of the American colonies. Burgoyne needed supplies badly for all his troops. He had a force of 10,000 men and camp attendants to feed. His scouts found a large store of beef, flour, and other supplies in Bennington, Vermont. They also reported that only a few hundred militiamen protected the small town. Burgoyne decided to send 700 men, mostly Hessians who, for lack of horses, had to travel by foot to try to confiscate the supplies. He chose German Lt. Colonel Friedrich Baum to lead the mission. American General John Stark learned of the approaching British and gathered his 2,000 New Hampshire and Massachusetts militiamen at Bennington on August 13, 1777.

Stark marched his men and some militiamen to the west of Bennington to prepare for battle. Heavy rains on the 15th prevented a battle that day, although Stark did send out **skirmishers**. The following morning, his troops were reinforced by the arrival of militia from Vermont and Massachusetts. Around noon, the rains stopped. At about 3 p.m., Stark began his attack. He had planned a four-fold assault: American troops would strike the enemy from the front, right, left, and rear. He called his men together in an inspiring call to action: "My men, yonder are the Hessians.... Tonight the American flag floats from yonder hill, or Molly Stark sleeps a widow."[18]

Stark's men were eager to fight and win. They began cheering and sending volley after volley at the enemy lines. Within two hours, most of Baum's troops ran for their lives as the shouting Americans pursued them through the woods in every direction. The Hessians on the hill put up a tremendous fight until they ran out of ammunition. They then attacked with their swords. Baum

skirmishers: Those who engage the enemy in light combat to delay their movement

was killed, and the Hessians, badly outnumbered, were surrounded. Many began to flee, and others surrendered, voluntarily becoming prisoners.

The Americans looked like they had achieved victory when Stark received an alarming report that Burgoyne had sent a force of 800 Hessians to reinforce Baum. They were only two miles away. The roads outside Bennington were like primitive paths, blocked with trees, underbrush, and rock. Also, American General Schuyler's men had purposely put obstacles in the way to deter progress by the British troops. The Hessians were only moving at half a mile an hour. Their artillery carts began to overturn in the rain-soaked earth, and the British guide became lost, causing them to take a long detour. However, General Stark was concerned that when the Hessians did arrive, it just might be too much for the Americans to handle, since Stark had his men scattered throughout the woods. Just in time, however, a regiment of Continental soldiers led by Seth Warner came to the rescue.

With his men now reinforced, Stark fended off the Hessians. Hearing gunfire, his scattered troops rushed to rejoin the main force. The Hessian soldiers were wearing heavy woolen uniforms. They were suffering from stifling humidity caused by the summer heat and rain. Stark's troops wore light linen shirts that allowed them to move freely in the oppressive air. After dark, the Hessian commander, realizing he was no match for Stark's troops, made a swift retreat to save his men from destruction.

Stark's men captured four cannons, along with wagons, horses, and muskets. It had been a brilliant American victory. Burgoyne's army had lost more than 900 men — 200 killed and 700 captured, in only one day. Stark's losses were 30 killed and 40 wounded. Burgoyne was stunned by the defeat. Up until then, he had been winning victory after victory. The loss of men and supplies Burgoyne suffered at Bennington contributed to his surrender two months later at the Battle of Saratoga.

John Hancock, president of the Continental Congress, wrote that the "brilliant victory gained by General Stark and Colonel Warner at Bennington gives the brightest luster to the American Army, and covers the enemies of the United States with Infamy and shame."[19] General Washington, in writing to General Israel Putnam, said, "As there is not now the least danger of Gen. Howe's going to New England, I hope the whole force of that Country will turn out and by following the great stroke struck by Gen. Stark near Bennington entirely crush Gen. Burgoyne."[20]

End of the War

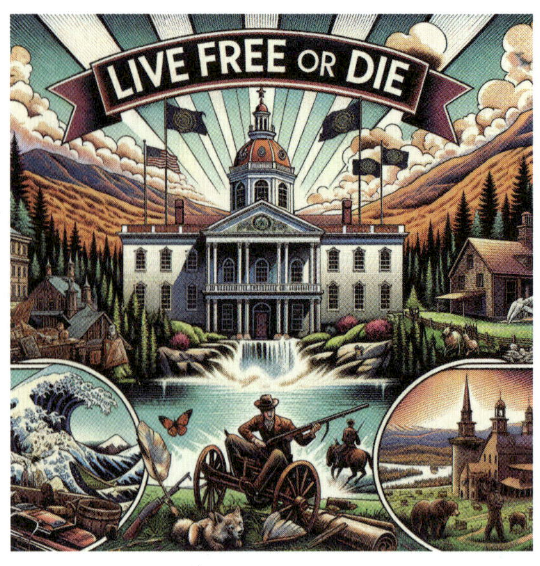

John Stark continued to fight courageously for the cause of independence. The War of Independence officially ended in September 1783 with the signing of the Treaty of Paris. John Stark had left the army the previous June because of a severe case of **rheumatism**. He went home to his large, happy family. For many years, the citizens of Bennington, Vermont, commemorated the Battle of Bennington on August 16. John wrote a letter for the occasion that was read each year. In 1809, he ended his letter with a **toast** reading, "Live Free or Die; Death is Not the Worst of Evils."[21] The first part of this toast would later be used as the New Hampshire state motto and be put on New Hampshire license plates.

rheumatism: Painful inflammation of joints

toast: A few words of remembrance

President Thomas Jefferson wrote in 1805, "The victories at Bennington — the first link in the chain of successes which issued in the surrender at Saratoga — are still fresh in the memory of every American and the name of him who achieved them dear to his heart."[22] At the time of his death in 1822, John Stark was the last surviving general of the American War of Independence.

5

Mad Anthony Wayne—The Midnight Attack

July 16, 1779	Stony Point, New York

The War of Independence was extremely difficult to win. The American Patriots were fighting against Great Britain, the most powerful nation in the world at that time. Great Britain had a large army and a powerful navy. America had only a small army and no navy when the war began. Washington needed a victory. He had been busy defending his army from British attacks and they had lost several battles. Many soldiers, hungry and poorly supplied with shoes and clothes, had given up and gone home. A victory was needed to give the men courage to fight on.

Who Was Anthony Wayne?

From the time he was a young boy, Anthony Wayne wanted to be a soldier. It occupied his thoughts most of the time. He attended a grade school taught by his Uncle Gilbert. His uncle wrote to Anthony's father expressing his concern that Anthony was not cut out to be a scholar, but perhaps a soldier. "He has already distracted the brains of two-thirds of the boys under my charge, by rehearsals of battles, sieges, etc. During noon in place of the usual games of amusement, he has the boys employed in throwing up redoubts,

skirmishes, etc."[23] He warned that if Anthony didn't begin paying more attention to book learning, he would have to **expel** him from school.

When his father read him the letter, Anthony demonstrated another quality of a good soldier, he was **submissive** authority. He put his mind to the task so thoroughly that in 18 months, his uncle said he had studied so well that he could instruct him no further. He was then sent to the academy in Philadelphia where he studied to be a **surveyor**. Surveying suited Anthony well, living in the wilderness, sleeping at night by a fire, and always being alert to the danger of attacks from the Native peoples. He was hired by Benjamin Franklin and others who owned land in Nova Scotia, to help families settle in the wild land of Nova Scotia. Anthony took his young wife Polly with him.

expel: Dismiss

submissive : Obedient

surveyor: One who measures land

Trouble Brewing

Anthony worked at this job for about a year, but trouble was brewing between the colonies and Great Britain. The job ended and Anthony and Polly came back to Waynesborough, Pennsylvania, where he was born and raised. Anthony became a member of the Committee of Safety. He began drilling troops and raising volunteers for the Pennsylvania militia. He read every book he could get his hands on to learn more about military tactics. Anthony inspired his men, assuring them that they would be fine soldiers and instilling in them a will to fight.

The Committee of Safety chose 30-year-old Anthony Wayne to be colonel of a regiment. He was sent to Canada with his men just in time to help the soldiers make a safe retreat amidst grueling fire. He was promoted to brigadier general for his service in the spring of 1777. When ordered to report to George Washington's headquarters, he was placed in command of the Pennsylvania Line, which amounted to one-fifth of the entire army.

The Soldier's General

Anthony Wayne was one of Washington's youngest generals in the War of Independence. His men loved his fervent spirit for victory and faithful attention to providing for their needs. Soon after the Battle of Brandywine, Wayne's men were dreadfully hungry. Since they were close to his farm in Waynesborough, he had six of his own cows slaughtered, giving his men the best meal they had eaten in a long time. At other times, he led expeditions to purchase cattle from surrounding towns to feed his men. His soldiers knew he would do whatever it took to care for them. One soldier remarked, "Ain't our Anthony Wayne a smart one? The other officers say, 'Too bad, there ain't no meat,' but our general goes out and gets it for us."[24] There were times he used his own money to purchase more clothing for his poorly-clad men.

Duty Calls

The Americans were defeated at the Battle of Brandywine. They were vastly outnumbered, and heavy fog concealed the British troops. Wayne's men fought hard to push the British back, but there were far too many Redcoats. Washington gave the order to retreat. Wayne and his men prevented the British from attacking until the rest of the American army was safely on the road before they joined them. At Germantown, Wayne was wounded twice and had his horse shot out from under him.

At the Battle of Monmouth, General Charles Lee proved a **coward** and began to retreat. When Washington came galloping up to where Lee was retreating and asked what was happening, a young drummer boy explained, "Mad Anthony is trying to fight the British army all by himself, and General Lee is retreating!"[25] Lee was **reprimanded** harshly and removed from duty, and Washington wrote a report to Congress **commending** Wayne's bravery. Anthony Wayne was involved in many campaigns of the war, from the wilds of Canada to the swamplands of the south, but he is best known for his last battle — the Battle of Stony Point.

coward: Person afraid of danger

reprimanded: Rebuked

commending: Praising

The Battle of Stony Point

The British had captured Stony Point, an American fort in New York. From this location, they could keep the American army from delivering troops and supplies, across the Hudson River. The Patriots desperately needed those supplies and there were not many other places where the river could be crossed. Washington decided to take back Stony Point. He chose Anthony Wayne to lead this attack. He was such a bold fighter and **tactical** genius that his men called him Mad Anthony Wayne. He loved a battle, but was also careful and alert to danger. He enthusiastically accepted the command.

The attack was carefully planned; however, it could only succeed if the British were completely surprised. Their advance would have to be under total silence. They would attack with bayonets to maintain silence, as the British had done during their surprise attack on General Wayne's troops at Paoli less than two years before. Near Paoli, a small town, Americans had tried to surrender, but many were cut down mercilessly by the British.

tactical: Strategic

General Wayne realized that he and his men had a hard fight ahead of them. The cliff around Stony Point was surrounded by two **barricades** of felled trees. Branches poking out from the limbs had been sharpened as spikes. Cannons at the top of the slope were sticking out of small holes in the stone fortress. About 1,300 men were selected who were well-skilled with the bayonet and known to be good fighters. The night

barricades: Blockades

before, Wayne walked among his troops, stopping by their campfires to speak words of encouragement to all his men. The first five men to enter the fort would get monetary rewards, and the first man would receive a promotion, too. Each man was given a piece of white paper to pin to his hat so he wouldn't be confused with the enemy in the heat of battle. No man was to utter a sound until the final order to attack, at which time they were all to shout, "The fort is ours."[26]

The Battle Is Won

Wayne divided his men into three groups. The only group with loaded muskets was to start the attack and engage the enemy, so the British would think this was the location of the main attack. While this was happening, the rest of the men would chop away the sharp logs surrounding the fort. Then the main body of troops would rush in through the gap. Just before midnight, orders were whispered and the troops began advancing. Stony Point was an island at high tide. Now, at half-tide, the soldiers had to wade in water above their waists, raising their muskets with fixed bayonets high above their heads. Men got busy chopping the first barricade with their axes. Wayne found a hole big enough to get his men through, though the sharpened branches tore at their shirts. They continued to climb.

Before they reached the second barricade, a British **fife** sounded an alarm from the top of the hill. Cannons

fife: Military flute

roared and muskets fired. Bullets flew all around them as two columns of men rushed the fort. The British were fooled, racing to where they heard guns firing, and responded with fierce fighting. Redcoat after Redcoat was struck down. In the midst of the fighting, Mad Anthony was struck in the head by a bullet and thought he was dying. “March on! Help me into the fort. Let me die at the head of the column!” he ordered.[27]

“The fort’s our own!” came the cry as the cannon stopped firing and the British flag was hauled down. Hundreds of British soldiers began surrendering, begging to be allowed to live. Wayne, wounded and lying on the dirt floor of the fort, heard their cries and remembered how his men had begged for mercy at Paoli, only to be struck down. He could have taken revenge for those actions at Paoli, but he would not. “Take prisoners,” he ordered, “every man who gives up his gun is to be spared.”[28] Sixty-three of the enemy were killed, 543 were taken prisoner, some of whom were wounded. The American losses were 15 killed and 83 wounded, mostly Wayne’s men who had been in the thick of the action. The Americans captured 15 good cannons and valuable supplies as well.

Wayne’s wound, fortunately, was only a scalp wound, and he recovered. The surgeon said if the bullet had struck a fraction of an inch lower, it would have killed him instantly.

Wayne was up at 2 a.m., requesting paper to write on. Leaning on his aides for support, he wrote a message to General Washington. "The fort and the garrison are ours. Our officers and men behaved like men determined to be free."[29]

The country was soon singing Wayne's praises. Congress sent him a medal; Washington praised him highly; many congratulated him. Most of all, the victory at Stony Point put new hope in the American people. The French gained confidence in the American cause as well. Benjamin Rush, a signer of the Declaration of Independence, praised Wayne for his decision to extend British soldiers mercy as soon as they requested it. "You have established the national character of our Country. You have taught our enemies, that bravery, humanity, and **magnanimity** are the national **virtues** of the Americans."[30]

The city of Fort Wayne, Indiana, bears Anthony Wayne's name, as do several counties, towns, parkways, a university, and many memorials. His hometown of Waynesborough still exists in Pennsylvania. At Valley Forge, there is a statue of General

magnanimity: Charity

virtues: Qualities

Anthony Wayne on horseback overlooking the country where "he played as a boy and which he defended as a man. His sword was sharp and his spirit bold and brave. He was one of our great fighters for freedom."[31]

6

John Sevier – The Battle of Kings Mountain

October 7, 1780	The War of Independence

In order for the British to have control of the southern colonies, they needed to secure the supply depots in the South. The largest of those supply posts was at Camden, South Carolina. In August 1780, it was under British authority. An American force led by Major Horatio Gates set out to capture it. Gates, however, was a poor field commander. The Americans, badly outnumbered, were trapped. Gates, as he had done at Saratoga, kept to the rear of his army while the fighting raged. It was one of the worst American defeats. Few Americans escaped, except for Gates, who fled on horseback.

This defeat left the British in temporary control of the southern colonies. However, there were some American leaders, rough and ready mountain men, driven to fight harder due to the tyranny and cruelty of the British soldiers and **Tories.** They were fighting because their houses were being burned, their cattle and horses were being stolen, and their families were living in constant threat of attack by Native Americans. They were **hardy** settlers and **staunch** Patriots. And they weren't afraid to fight!

Tories: American colonists who supported the British side

hardy: Accustomed to hardship

staunch: Firm

Who Was John Sevier?

John Sevier was born in the beautiful Shenandoah Valley of Virginia in 1745. He was taught to read by his mother and later attended the academy at Staunton, Virginia. He did well at school, but his passion was being outdoors. He loved hunting squirrels, turkeys, foxes, or deer, and was skilled in riding horses. When his school days were over, he went home and became a clerk at his father's store. He earned a reputation for honesty and was respected by all who knew him.

John married Sarah Hawkins, his childhood friend, when he was 16 years old. They had a happy marriage. They eventually had ten children together. John bought a tract of land in the Shenandoah Valley and founded a little town that he named New Market. That town still exists today.

Sevier built a store, the only one around, and many people came to buy dry goods, groceries, and other supplies. By the age of 26, he was a successful businessman. He gave the local Baptist church three acres of land to build a church for the community. John Sevier loved people. He would do anything he could to help them. He also had a genius for military leadership. Frontiersmen would undergo any

hardship necessary to do what he asked of them. The governor made him captain of the militia under Colonel George Washington because he had earned a reputation for protecting families from attacks by Native peoples.

Moving West

Sevier heard about a band of pioneers building a settlement near the Watauga River, which was a settlement area south of the Holston River, on the Watauga and Nolichucky Rivers in the colony of North Carolina. This area later became the state of Tennessee. After visiting the settlement, he decided to move his family there. They arrived on Christmas Day, 1773. The settlers helped their neighbors do whatever was necessary. If a new house had to be built, they all helped to build it. If a field needed to be cleared, they all pitched in to make short work of it. And when it came time to stockpile wood for the winter, they had a "chopping bee" to get the work done in record time.

The Sevier family would read in the evenings — books they had brought and shared with neighbors, and always the Bible. They would sing hymns together by the fire. Whenever there was trouble with horse thieves or other dangers, the men looked to John Sevier for leadership. He became clerk of the court and later was elected to be a judge because his neighbors loved and trusted him.

Surprise Attack

When the colonies declared independence from Great Britain, the British bribed the Cherokee people, giving them guns and ammunition and encouraging them to fight the colonists. The Cherokees planned a surprise attack on Fort Watauga. They came sneaking up early one morning through the woods near the fort. The colonists were on guard as always. When the first shots rang out, the colonists fled to the fort for protection but had to leave their livestock and food stores in their haste.

Some of the women of the settlement had been milking the cows when shots were fired. They ran to the fort for protection, but the gates closed before one of them, Katherine Sherrill, could reach it. Seeing her running, some of the Native people ran out of the woods to capture her. John Sevier, on top of the wall of the fort, saw Katherine's **peril** and called to her to run faster. He shot the man chasing her who was closest behind her.

peril: Danger

Then, as she jumped for the top of the wall, John reached down and pulled her over. She fell into his arms. Later, after John's beloved wife died, he fell in love with and married Katherine, "Bonny Kate," as he called her. The siege lasted for three weeks before the fighting was over and the colonists were safe again for the time being.

Moving Again

In 1778, John again moved his family, this time to the Nolichucky Settlement. He bought a tract of land he called Mount Pleasant. He got the nickname "Nolichucky Jack" because of this move. It was peaceful for a while, although John still had to act as a **scout** to look out for the movements of the Native peoples. He had built his house of huge, heavy logs with large fireplaces and rooms for guests. Here he and Sarah entertained friends and strangers. Settlers from all over would enjoy hominy, cornbread, and wild meat of many kinds in the Sevier home. It was here that Sarah died in 1780. In August of the same year, John married "Bonny Kate," whom he had rescued from the Native Americans four years before. Kate bore eight more children. John was always a loving father. Sometimes John and Kate invited neighbors in for barbecues. They never turned away a stranger. "Nolichucky Jack, as his neighbors loved to call him, held a warm place in every settler's heart."[32]

scout: Person who gathers information

Cornwallis' Plan

In 1780, British General Charles Cornwallis sent Colonel Patrick Ferguson with 1,000 British soldiers into Western North Carolina to "punish" the backwoodsmen. The British were greatly annoyed by **skirmishes** from the backwoodsmen. The British commander had tasked two of his officers — Banastre Tarleton and Ferguson — to **pillage** farms, raise and train troops from among the Tories, and break up bands of armed Patriots. Ferguson made a huge mistake when he sent a messenger to Colonel Issac Shelby, threatening that "if the backwoodsmen did not quit resisting the royal arms, he would march his army over the mountains, and would straightway lay waste their homes with fire and sword and hang their leaders."[33]

skirmishes: Unexpected, irregular fighting

pillage: Steal from and destroy

Colonel Shelby of Kentucky rode immediately to John Sevier's home 60 miles away, to tell him of Ferguson's threat. When Shelby arrived, Sevier was hosting a barbecue, roasting an ox on a spit. The colonel told his story to all the guests. Sevier resolved to call the frontiersmen together, cross the mountains, and teach Colonel Ferguson a lesson. The barbecue was over, and the men attending agreed to join Sevier. These rugged mountaineers took Ferguson's threat seriously. Shelby left to muster his own men. He sent word to Colonel William Campbell, another famous frontier fighter who lived 40 miles

away in Holston, Virginia, to call out his men. They were to all meet at Sycamore Shoals on the Watauga River on September 25.

Colonel Sevier tried without success to borrow money to equip the men with horses and supplies. The people would have been willing to give their last dollar, but they had paid out all their money for land, and the cash was in the hands of the county entry taker, John Adair. When a person claimed a tract of land, it was known as an entry. At the time of entry, all fees had to be paid. The entry taker collected the funds and then issued a warrant to the county surveyor to survey the land. Sevier appealed to him. This was his reply:

> "I have no authority by law, Col. Sevier, to make that disposition of this money. It belongs to the treasury of North Carolina and I dare not appropriate a penny of it to any purpose. But if the country is overrun by the British, liberty is gone. Let the money go, too. Take it. If the enemy by its use is driven from the country, I can trust that country to justify and vindicate by conduct. Take it."[34]

The money amounted to $13,000 in silver and gold. Sevier purchased the supplies.

The entire military force met at Sycamore Shoals. It was decided that the younger men would march while the older men would stay to help the women defend their homes in case of attacks. Women came to say goodbye to husbands, fathers, and brothers, bringing blankets, horses, guns, and food. One thousand backwoodsmen mounted on horses, clothed in fringed hunting shirts and coonskin caps, long rifles in hand, began the march from Watauga across the mountains. They were joined by several hundred North Carolinians.

The Battle of Kings Mountain

Early on the morning of September 26, the little army was prepared for battle. They all met to hear their minister, Rev. Samuel Doak, pray for the success of their mission. Years before, this God-fearing man had crossed the mountains with his horse loaded with Bibles. He had founded churches and schools and had a positive influence on these frontier people. Every man **reverently** bowed his head and listened while the old preacher **fervently** "prayed that they might stand bravely in battle and that the sword of the Lord and of Gideon might smite their foes."[35] Colonel Shelby told the men if any wanted to go home, this was their chance. Not one man chose to leave.

reverently: With respect

fervently: Passionately

Colonel Ferguson was trying to keep out of the way of the Patriots while waiting for the Tories to reinforce his troops. On October 6, Ferguson retreated to Kings Mountain. The ridge where he set up camp was nearly a half-mile long and 60 feet above the valley. Its steep sides were covered in timber; one side was too steep to climb at all. There he waited with 1,000 men armed with bayonets. He **arrogantly** boasted that he could never be driven from the ridge by all the rebels or even by God Himself.

The backwoodsmen chose 900 men to charge up the mountain. They knew they would have to face British bayonets, although not one of them owned a bayonet. Three divisions of mountain men, one for each side, began their climb. Colonel Sevier led the right wing. Some of his men, riding quickly, got to the rear of Ferguson's troops, cutting off their only chance for retreat. All the divisions moved so fast that Ferguson was surrounded in short order. The Patriots were **dodging** bayonets as they moved **stealthily** from tree to tree, jumping out to fire and then taking cover behind another tree.

arrogantly: Proudly

dodging: Moving to avoid

stealthily: Cautiously so they wouldn't be seen

The British were now being shot at from both sides as well as in front. Ferguson sent messengers to ask Cornwallis to send more troops, but there wasn't time for help to arrive. The backwoodsmen were skilled and hardly ever missed their targets.

The British retreated to the top of the mountain. Ferguson's men were falling fast. Both sides fought like tigers. Ferguson concentrated his forces to attempt to destroy Sevier's division, but the Americans were the first to appear at the top of the ridge. They drove Ferguson's men into a group around the supply wagons.

Some of the British soldiers began to hold up white flags of surrender, but Ferguson dashed up to the flags and cut them down with his sword, vowing he would never surrender. His second-in-command begged him to give up, but Ferguson refused. He dashed his horse into Sevier's line, cutting and slashing with his sword until it actually broke. Several of Sevier's men took aim at Ferguson. He fell from his horse, dead. His entire army was either captured or killed. Only 28 Patriots were killed and 60 wounded.

The whole battle was over in about an hour. Sevier's men were rewarded with a meal of British rations before heading back over the mountains. The Americans were overjoyed! The victory of the Battle of Kings Mountain helped stop the tide of British success in the South.

After the War

Finally, the war was over, and the colonists were free. John Sevier and others set up a new government and called it the state of Franklin, after Benjamin Franklin. Its name was changed to Tennessee when the territory officially became a state. The people elected John Sevier as governor. The citizens' support of this bold pioneer was so great that he held his office for 12 years. In 1811, he was elected congressman from Tennessee. John Sevier died in 1815 when he was surveying land the United States had purchased from the Creek peoples. His grave is now at the Knox County Courthouse in Knoxville, Tennessee. "Bonny Kate" rests beside him. For generations, the children of pioneers have told their children the story of the courage and goodness of "Nolichucky Jack." He was a perfect example of what it means to be an American.

7

Reverend James Caldwell – The Fighting Chaplain

1780–1781	Elizabethtown, New Jersey

In late November 1779, General George Washington decided that the Continental Army would return to a familiar location for winter camp. He chose Morristown, New Jersey, where they had spent the winter of 1776 to 1777. In the summer of 1780, a large British force crossed from Staten Island, New York, to Elizabethtown, New Jersey, intending to drive Washington from his camp at Morristown.

Who Was Reverend James Caldwell?

James Caldwell was born on April 14, 1734, in Charlotte County, Virginia. He graduated from Princeton College in 1759 and was licensed to preach in 1760. He was offered a congregation in Elizabethtown, New Jersey, and moved there to pastor. His father had come to this country for religious freedom, and James "inherited a spirit of independence and of resistance to tyranny which made him from the outset of our troubles enlist his heart and soul in the cause of American independence."[36]

Among his church members were staunch patriots such as William Livingston, the first governor of New Jersey, Abraham

Clark, one of the signers of the Declaration of Independence, and Elias Boudinot, who became president of the Continental Congress. Both the pastor and his congregation were regarded as head Patriot leaders of the province and disliked by the **Loyalists**. They "formed a band of noble men, of which New Jersey is justly proud."[37] On March 14, 1763, Reverend Caldwell married Hannah Ogden, a descendant of the Pilgrims. Together they raised ten children. He was thoroughly devoted to his family, his congregation, and his Lord.

Loyalists: Those loyal to Great Britain

Call to Duty

When trouble arose with Great Britain, New Jersey called up a regiment. Reverend Caldwell was elected to be its chaplain. On the Sabbath, he would preach to his congregation; the next day, he'd be in the army, often traveling the country collecting valuable information for the Patriots. He recruited 31 officers and 52 enlisted men from his church. He did everything he could to acquire weapons, shoes, and supplies for the needy troops, often paying for them from his own resources. He was appointed Assistant Commissary General. People trusted in his integrity so much that provisions began to come in from the citizens of New Jersey.

Reverend Caldwell permitted his church to be used as a hospital for the sick and wounded soldiers. He and Hannah often cared for the wounded there. Caldwell's activities became known to the British, who offered large rewards for his capture, just as they had done for Governor Livingston. The British knew where he lived. When they took over Staten Island, Caldwell decided to move his family to safety. He chose Connecticut Farms, a small village near Elizabethtown. Whenever he preached, he would place a pistol on each side of his Bible, and a row of muskets would be in the front of the church, ready for instant use.

Safety Threatened

In January 1780, the British burned his church to the ground. Reverend Caldwell, watching the smoldering ashes of the church, said to his militia, "Never mind, boys. We are fighting the noblest cause for which men ever fought. Never fear. The British made a big mistake. They misjudged us, thinking we were tired of fighting and ready to support King George. Nothing could be farther from the truth."[38]

In June, General Knyphausen (a German commander known for his cruelty) and his troops arrived in New Jersey. Reverend Caldwell was awakened early by a messenger with news that the enemy was approaching. He mounted his horse and left quickly, but turned back, fearing for his family's safety. His wife asked why he was back, and he told her he wanted her and the children to accompany him to camp. He felt uneasy leaving them. Hannah, realizing they would greatly slow him down, calmly refused to leave, saying she had no apprehensions for her own safety. Surely the British wouldn't harm a woman and her children. She brought him a cup of coffee, and while he sat on his horse drinking it, the enemy showed up. He bid her a hasty goodbye and "commending her to the care of the God in whom they both trusted, he struck his spurs into his horse and dashed away."[39]

Hannah Is Killed

Reverend Caldwell hadn't been gone long when Hannah began to regret her decision not to leave as he had begged her. She heard women and children screaming, running through the streets. She feared the British were on a **rampage**. She took eight-month-old Maria and her other children to her bedroom to pray. Hannah's maid, helping her with the children, looked out the window to see a "red coat" jump over the fence into the yard. The soldier, peering through her window, raised his rifle and fired, killing Hannah instantly. Other soldiers rushed into the house, slashed open Hannah's dress, and snatched her

rampage: Violent or excited behavior that is reckless or destructive

jewelry. They then set fire to the house along with the whole village as they left. The housekeeper, Abigail Lennington, screamed for some of the neighbors, who rescued the terrified Caldwell children. They also managed to drag Hannah's lifeless body outside before the flames reached it.

James Hears the News

James Caldwell was on a hillside with the Marquis de Lafayette and the army, ministering to the troops, when he saw smoke rising. He commented to Lafayette, "Thank God the fire is not in the direction of my house."[40] That evening, however, he heard two soldiers whispering something about Mrs. Caldwell. When he asked what they were saying, they hesitated; then told him what had happened. He breathed a short prayer and turned away to weep. Fearing for his children's safety, he hurried to find them. The once quiet little village was in charred ruins. A neighbor woman placed baby Maria in his arms and said, "You must live for your children and for your country. They both need you."[41]

After burying Hannah's body at the Presbyterian church graveyard in Elizabethtown, he left his children in the care of parishioners and headed back to the army. Reverend James Caldwell said of his wife, Hannah, "She was of so sweet a temper, so prudent, benevolent, and soft in her manners, that I verily believe she had not upon earth one personal enemy."[42]

Citizens Enraged

The British had hoped to dishearten the population, but Hannah's death had the opposite effect. Men were inspired to join the militia in overwhelming numbers. George Washington praised them for their response:

> It roused the indignation of the whole community — filling all with one spirit: to avenge the deed and drive the invaders from the soil! It animated the brave with new energy, inspired the timid to feats of heroism and determined the irresolute to throng to the standard of liberty. The Caldwell tragedy raised the resolution of the country to the highest pitch.[43]

The Battle of Springfield

After burning Connecticut Farms, the enemy advanced toward Springfield, determined to cause destruction there as well. Washington had previously set a cannon (nick-named the "Old Sow" by the soldiers) and a tar barrel on a pole at a high point by Springfield. The flaming tar barrel at night would be the call to arms. By day, the boom of the cannon warned all within earshot that the enemy was coming.

On June 23, the militia and farmers came running at the sound of the cannon fire. Reverend Caldwell was engaged in the heaviest fighting when one of the companies ran out of wadding for their guns. Wadding was paper necessary to hold the musketball in place. Without it, they could not fire their muskets. Caldwell galloped over to the nearby Presbyterian church, rushed inside, and began grabbing hymnbooks from the pews. Racing back to the battle, he began throwing hymnbooks — most of the songs in them composed by Isaac Watts — to all the soldiers, calling out, "Give 'em Watts, boys! Now put Watts into them, boys!"[44]

The men began tearing out pages, ramming home the charges, and giving the British "Watts" with vigor. Over the next two days, the militia helped Continental troops drive back a British force five times their size, forcing the British to retreat and winning the Battle of Springfield. George Washington praised the militia, "They flew to arms universally and acted with a spirit equal to anything I have seen in the war."[45]

Many credit the patriotic fervor of "The Fighting Chaplain" for the success of the battle. Reverend Caldwell had a gift for encouraging his troops in battle when all seemed lost. "The darker the prospects became, the higher rose his resolution. The more complicated and disheartening the condition of the army grew, the more persevering were his efforts…."[46] Caldwell was always reminding the troops amidst all the horrors of war, "Jehovah reigns … and all will be well."[47] The British never achieved their goal of reaching Morristown, and the Battle of Springfield was the last time the British invaded New Jersey.

James Caldwell Dies

There was a Quaker family living in New York by the name of Murray who had shown much kindness to Jersey prisoners held in that city. On November 24, one of the family, Miss Beulah Murray, came to visit relatives at Elizabethtown under a flag of **truce**. Reverend Caldwell took his carriage down to meet and escort her to town. There was a sentry guarding the fort at Elizabethtown Point. Caldwell tied up his horse, went to the wharf, and helped Miss Murray to his carriage. He then went back to the boat to pick up her belongings. The sentry ordered him to stop, probably wanting to search the bundle. Americans worried about illegal British goods being brought into New Jersey. Caldwell stopped and was about to open the bundle when the sentry shot him. Caldwell slumped to the ground, dead.

truce: Agreement to stop fighting

The man who shot him was James Morgan, a member of the Jersey militia. His motive isn't known for sure, but is commonly believed that he was bribed by the British to slay Caldwell. He was tried, convicted of murder, and hung.

At Caldwell's funeral, Elias Boudinot walked the Caldwell children up to the coffin of their father and made a heartfelt appeal for folks to adopt them. Each was adopted by a fine family, and all of them became useful, distinguished members of society as adults. One son was adopted by Marquis de Lafayette. He was raised in France and, as an adult, returned to the United States to found "The Christian Herald." Another son became an important judge in New Jersey. Another became clerk of the U.S. Supreme Court and later a Presbyterian minister like his father. A daughter became the wife of the President of Athens College in Georgia.

Both James and Hannah are buried on the grounds of Elizabethtown Presbyterian Church, where he was the pastor. A monument was erected there. It says, "This monument is erected to the memory of Rev. James Caldwell, the pious and fervent preacher, and a prominent leader among the worthies who secured the independence of this country. His name will be cherished in the Church and in the State so long as virtue is esteemed and patriotism honored."[48]

8

Nathanael Greene – The Fighting Quaker

1780–1781	Virginia, North Carolina, Georgia, South Carolina

Although the first battles of the War of Independence took place in the Northeast, the British saw it would be difficult to defeat the Patriots there. They believed if they could get the Loyalists in the South to join their army and fight their neighbors, the strength of their army would increase. So they turned their attention to Virginia, North Carolina, South Carolina, and Georgia. After General Gates led the American army during a tremendous defeat at Camden, South Carolina, in August 1780, George Washington knew he must replace Gates with a new general.

Who Was Nathanael Greene?

Nathanael Greene was born in Warwick, Rhode Island, in 1742. His father was a farmer, a grist mill owner who ground grain, a blacksmith, and on Sundays, a Quaker preacher. He trained his son to be a strict Quaker, and Quakers didn't believe in going to war. Nathanael's father taught him to work in the field and the **forge**. Nathanael, however, loved to learn. He studied whenever he had spare time. Mr. Greene had a reputation for crafting ship anchors at his forge. As a boy, Nathanael earned spending money by making

forge: Furnace for shaping metal

miniature anchors and other toys there. With the money he earned, he bought books. When he was a young man, he met Reverend Ezra Stiles, who would eventually become president of Yale University. Reverend Stiles encouraged young Nathanael to keep reading books. Whenever Nathanael could go to town, he would visit the reverend and talk with him about whatever he was learning.

When it became evident in 1774 that a war was brewing, Nathanael Greene helped organize a militia in Rhode Island — a very unusual thing for a Quaker man to do. He obtained books about military strategy and studied constantly. Being a Quaker, he didn't own a musket, so he had to go to Boston to buy one. While there, he watched recruits for the militia training so he could learn more about military drills. He hid the gun under some hay in his wagon to avoid confiscation by the British.

War Begins

As soon as news of the Battles of Lexington and Concord was heard, Rhode Island raised three **regiments**. Since Greene had shown great military skill and

regiments: Companies of soldiers

leadership, he was promoted to Brigadier General. He sat down to write a letter to his wife Kitty, explaining he would much rather be with her at their peaceful home, but that duty called to help secure that peace.

> … But the injury done my country, and the chains of slavery forging for our posterity, calls me forth to defend our common rights and repel the bold invaders of the sons of freedom. I hope the righteous God that rules the world will bless the armies of America and receive of those whose lot it is to fall in action into the paradise of God and into whose protection I commend you and myself, and am with the truest regard, your loving husband, N. Greene.[49]

He left immediately for Boston. There he met General George Washington, who had just arrived to take command of the army. Thirty-three-year-old General Greene had the honor of welcoming Washington on behalf of all the soldiers. Greene was made one of Washington's generals and followed his commander through many engagements of the war. He became a dear and trusted friend of Washington, who was confident of his leadership and gave him new responsibilities. Washington told Congress that Greene was "a Gentleman in whom I place the most entire confidence."[50] When Washington needed a general to try to win back the South from Cornwallis, Greene was his choice.

War in the South

When Greene arrived in the Carolinas, he found the army in bad shape. There was only one blanket to be shared by every three men. Food was always scarce. The soldiers were very discouraged because they had lost so many battles and also because they were often unpaid. Many men were sick. Greene went to work doing his best to build the confidence of his men by caring for their needs. Greene knew that regardless of the condition of the troops, they would fight if given a chance. It was these men who had just killed or captured 1,000 British soldiers at King's Mountain. Not only that, but Greene had some of the bravest leaders to help him. Among them were Daniel Morgan, Francis Marion, William Washington (cousin of George), Henry Lee (Lighthorse Harry), and Thomas Sumter. They would prevail with God's help.

Greene divided his army into two divisions. He marched into northeastern South Carolina with 1,000 men. Marion and Lee, with small groups of cavalries, sneaked up on the British outposts. Charging in broad daylight into Georgetown, they captured the officer in charge and got away before the British could react. Greene sent Morgan and William Washington with 900 men into northwestern South Carolina to threaten British outposts and encourage Patriots in the mountains. At about the same time, General Washington surprised a party of British soldiers, capturing 250 of them.

Morgan's Men

Lord Cornwallis was at his wits' end now and determined to put an end to such losses. He ordered the fearsome Colonel Banastre Tarleton with his 1,100 soldiers to capture Daniel Morgan and his men. Morgan was not the type to be taken by surprise, however. He was known for his fierce fighting in the French and Indian War. Once, with a company of 96 Virginia backwoodsmen, he had marched 600 miles in just 21 days to join General Washington in Boston. Later, Washington sent him to join in the capture of Burgoyne at Saratoga. Burgoyne expressed admiration for the skillful fighting of Morgan's men: "Sir, you command the finest regiment in the world!"[51]

Hearing of Tarleton's advance, Morgan gathered his men at Cowpens, which he knew would be a good location for fighting. He placed Continental troops on top of a long, steep slope. Colonel Washington and his men held the rear. The militiamen were in front of the Continentals with orders not to retreat until each soldier had fired twice. In front of the militia, Morgan placed a troop of skilled sharpshooters hiding in the woods on both the right and left sides.

With great confidence, Tarleton's men arrived, thinking this would be an easy victory. But the militia fired, not only twice but several times before retreating behind the Continentals, who began pouring deadly fire into the approaching British troops. Just then, Colonel Washington's troops charged out and struck the right flank of the Redcoats. The militia, having reloaded, made a dash and struck the left flank. Most of Tarleton's men immediately threw down their arms in surrender. Only 270 British soldiers managed to escape. Tarleton came close to being wounded by Colonel Washington.

The defeat of Tarleton enraged Cornwallis. Destroying all his heavy baggage, he pursued Morgan, who wisely left for the banks of the Catawba River, where he met up with Greene and his army. Combining forces, they headed for the Yadkin River. The ingenious Greene had brought boats mounted on light wheels so they could be pulled on the roads by horses. When they came to a river, the boats floated across with the wheels hanging underneath, making the crossing easy. Cornwallis' men, however, had to march up the river until his army could find a spot shallow enough to wade across. Greene was already well on his way to the Dan River, which crossed into Virginia.

When Cornwallis reached the river, the heavy rains had made the water too deep and swift for safe passage. The Americans had used all the boats in the area to cross the river and were safely on the other side when the British arrived. Greene had won the race! The two parts of his army were now together and could rest for a few days without danger of attack.

The Battle of Guilford Courthouse

General Greene had won a great victory by successfully retreating. His army was growing stronger every day as hundreds more men joined them. Cornwallis was stuck hundreds of miles away from his supplies and **reinforcements**. A few weeks later, when the river receded, Greene had his army cross back into North Carolina to attack Cornwallis at Guilford Courthouse. Greene divided his men into three parallel lines on the road where the British would advance. In front of the first line, he had blocked the road with two light pieces of artillery. In the stifling heat at noon, the British showed up. Greene had his men fire on them immediately. He rode through his troops calling, "Steady now! Stand firm, and you can finish it! Our fire is taking effect!"[52]

reinforcements: More volunteers

Cornwallis' horse had been killed under him, and he had remounted on one of his men's animals. When he emerged from the woods on his new horse, he saw what appeared to be a British retreat. He ordered his artillery to open at close range, firing ammunition into the middle of the fight. Thousands of bullets claimed lives, both

American and British, in Cornwallis' outrageous attempt to drive back the Patriots! One of his generals, though wounded himself, protested frantically that they were destroying their own men. More than one British officer turned his face away, sickened at the sight. Cornwallis, however, said he found it a necessary act of war. British cannons fired again and again, mowing down Redcoats and Americans **indiscriminately**.

Greene rode forward to get a better look. His aide caught his horse's bridle, turning him back toward the Courthouse, to protect his general from being shot. Greene was astonished and sickened that the British general would cruelly turn his cannons on his own men. Determined not to add to his losses, Greene called for a retreat to his old encampment on Troublesome Creek. Lord Cornwallis left all his wounded to the compassion of General Greene. One-fourth of Cornwallis' army had been killed or wounded. Greene's losses were much less than

indiscriminately: Randomly

those of Cornwallis. The troops were exhausted but not discouraged.

In a letter to a friend in Congress, Greene wrote, "We were obliged to give up the ground, and left our artillery; but the enemy has been so soundly beaten that they dare not move towards us since the action, notwithstanding that we lay within ten miles of them for ten days. We have little to eat, less to drink, and lodge in the woods in the midst of smoke. Our fatigue is great. I was so much overcome night before last that I fainted."[53] Greene pursued the retreating Redcoats as far as Ramsay's Mill on the Haw River. Realizing he was now the pursued instead of the pursuer, Cornwallis departed his camp so quickly that he left whole quarters of freshly cut beef. Greene's hungry men were revived by the best meal they had eaten in many weeks. After the disastrous "victory" at Guilford Courthouse, Cornwallis retreated to Wilmington and remained there 18 days to let his army rest. Soon thereafter he set up camp at Yorktown, only to be surrounded and trapped by the American army.

Determined General

Greene turned back to South Carolina, where the British still held Charleston and a few other towns. He wrote to Washington that he was determined to carry the war back to South Carolina, "which would be unexpected to the enemy and force him to follow or give up all his posts in that state."[54] Greene fought more battles — some he lost and some he won, but he never gave up. "We fight, get beat, rise, and fight again," he often told his men.[55] The British lost so many men at the Battles of Eutaw Springs and Hobkirks Hill that they were forced to retreat to Charleston. That's where those troops were when news from Yorktown ended the serious fighting. The war in the South had been won by the Quaker general from Rhode Island against "Britain's battle-hardened regulars led by the best general in the field."[56] America was a free nation.

General Greene's work as a soldier was done. Congress presented him with a medal for the Battle of Eutaw Springs and gave him a large sum of money. He sold some of his land to help pay debts he had accumulated from buying supplies

for his men during the Southern campaigns. The state of Georgia gave him a large plantation on the Savannah River where he eventually moved with his family. He was offered the job of Secretary of War twice, but he turned it down. He remained a faithful Patriot until his death at the age of 43 in 1786.

9

Emily Geiger – A Dangerous Ride

June 1781	South Carolina

It was the summer of 1781. The American colonies were in the thick of a terrible war. Colonial Patriots were fighting for their independence from the most powerful country in the world — Great Britain. Some colonists, called Tories, still loyal to the British crown, were causing much trouble for the Patriots. In South Carolina, two American generals were leading the Patriot army: General Nathanael Greene and General Thomas Sumter. General Greene had been capturing British forts all across South Carolina. One, however, Fort Ninety Six, had proved too strong to be taken. General Greene needed to come up with a plan to capture that one as well.

Who Was Emily Geiger?

Emily Geiger was the 18-year-old daughter of a wealthy farmer who lived in Lexington, South Carolina. The family members were Patriots, but her father, John, was confined to bed, too ill to fight. Their farmhouse was situated about two miles from the American camp. One morning their neighbor rode over to explain a desperate situation to Emily's father. General Nathanael Greene was returning from an unsuccessful 28-day assault on the British fort at Ninety Six. He had just learned that British Lord

Rawdon had divided his troops. Greene believed that if he could add General Sumter's forces to his own, he might stand a chance of defeating Rawdon and perhaps manage to capture Fort Ninety Six. Sumter was 100 miles away, across a wild stretch of country full of British and Tory scouts, not to mention wild animals. He desperately needed to get word to him, but how? Anyone who took on such a dangerous mission would run the risk of being captured and probably hanged.

Emily Volunteers

As Emily listened to her neighbor, she began to devise a plan. Ever since the start of the war, she had been wishing there was something she could do to help the cause of liberty. She knew she couldn't grab a gun and fight in place of her sick father. But there was something she could do! General Greene needed someone to deliver a vitally important message to General Sumter. General Greene hesitated to order any of his men, who were exhausted and weak from lack of proper food, to undertake such a ride.

Emily knew the road well. She often traveled on it to visit her uncle's family. If stopped, she could say she was going for a visit. Also, the British would be less likely to suspect a woman. She promptly got her horse and headed for Greene's encampment. The general was **pondering** what to do when a messenger informed him that a young woman

> **pondering:** Thinking about

was waiting to see him. Emily told the general of her plan, explaining that she had taken the route many times to visit her Uncle Jacob. General Greene told her the mission was much too dangerous for her. It would take days, and Tory spies were on the lookout all over that territory.

Emily pleaded again, stating why she thought she could succeed. He finally agreed, **reluctantly**, as he could not think of any other way to get his message through. He took out a sheet of paper and began to write his message to General Sumter, explaining his plan. Then he went over and over it with Emily until he was sure she had memorized every word. This way, if the British should stop and question her, she should destroy the message and deliver it verbally to General Sumter if she managed to make it through safely. Emily hid the letter in the front of her dress.

reluctantly: Hesitatingly

The Journey

Emily immediately left for home. She unsaddled her horse and flung the saddle over her father's horse, the fastest one in the stable. As she rode away, she noticed her

Tory neighbor, Lowry, watching her and had a little pang of fear. Four hours later, a fellow Tory who had been spying in Greene's camp came to inform Lowry that Emily had gone to deliver a message to Sumter's camp. Lowry decided to send the man on to catch her.

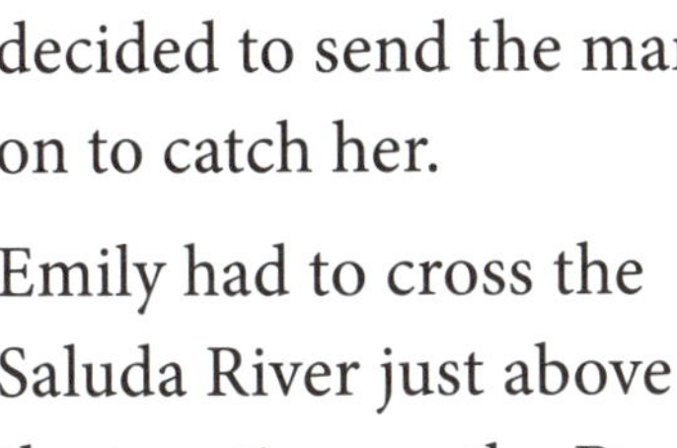

Emily had to cross the Saluda River just above the junction on the Broad River. She rode all day. When it began to get dark, she knew she had to find a place to spend the night. It was dangerous to ride through the woods at night. She found a farmhouse and was politely invited in by the farmer and his wife. When asked where she was headed, she told them she was visiting her uncle. The couple warmly welcomed her, stabled her horse, and offered her food and shelter. That night at supper the couple warned Emily to beware of Greene's men who were in the woods. Emily realized that they were Tories!

Night Escape

In the middle of the night, Emily woke to the sound of voices. A man was talking to the farmer and his wife. Emily was only able to hear bits of the conversation, but what she heard frightened her. Lowry, her Tory neighbor, had sent a spy, Billy Mink, to track her down. Mink, thinking she was sound asleep and being weary himself, decided to sleep awhile and capture her in the morning. Emily lay frozen until the voices stopped and she was sure they were all asleep. She got up, tiptoed to the window, and jumped quietly to the ground. A dog ran up to her, but she bent over and spoke soothingly to him, petting him on the head to keep him from barking. Emily quickly saddled her horse and galloped away. She left by way of a field to **muffle** the sound of her horse's feet. She remembered her own words to General Greene that a woman can pass where a man cannot. She tried to ignore the nighttime shadows and sounds of owls, bobcats, and coyotes around her. She had to think only of the importance of her mission and keep up her courage.

muffle: Make quieter

Emily rode for hours, pushing her horse as fast as she dared. As the sun began to rise, she had covered about two-thirds of the 100 miles to Sumter's camp. Suddenly, as she was passing through the thick hardwoods near Friday's Ferry on the Congaree River, three of Lord Rawdon's Tory scouts burst out of the forest and surrounded her horse. They noticed that her horse was covered with sweat from heavy riding and that she had been coming from the direction of General Greene's camp. "Where are you going?" they demanded. "I'm on my way to my uncle's house," she told them. Emily's cheeks however turned a bright, rosy color. Looking at her blushing face, they did not believe her. They concluded she must be on a secret mission. They brought her to Lord Rawdon's camp at Fort Granby, a mile away.

Questioned

The soldiers took Emily to a tiny room on the upper level of the guardhouse and locked her in. British rule didn't allow a man to search a woman spy. They knew they must find a woman to see if Emily carried a message. Someone hurried off to find a Tory woman. Emily took advantage of the delay. She took the message out of her dress and read it over again to refresh her mind. She knew if someone found it, her life would be in great danger. She ripped it into pieces and began to chew and swallow them, one by one. The paper nearly choked her, but she almost managed to finish chewing just before the door opened, and a woman entered. She threw herself down on the nearby bed. Covering her face with her hands so the woman wouldn't see her chew the last piece, she pretended to cry.

The old Tory woman, Mrs. Hogabook, soothed the sobbing girl, assuring her that no one would harm her. Then she searched Emily from head to foot. She was kind but very thorough. If Emily had not eaten the message, it would surely have been found. But Mrs. Hogabook found nothing. She scolded Lord Rawdon's men for **detaining** and searching the girl. She told them it was disgraceful to put the girl through such an embarrassing experience. The commanding officer of the scouts apologized, and then in order to make **amends**, he gave Emily an **escort** to her uncle's home.

On with the Mission

As it was getting late in the day, Emily spent the night there but left early in the morning. She took a roundabout way, riding on some old paths to avoid being stopped again. Finally, at three in the afternoon of the third day, Emily rode out of the woods onto a traveled road. There, to her great relief, she saw Continental soldiers drilling. Emily excitedly told the men she had a critical, time-sensitive message for

detaining: Delaying

amends: Make up for wrongdoing

escort: Someone to accompany her

General Sumter from General Greene. The men took Emily straight to General Sumter's camp on the Wateree River. Emily, dusty and exhausted, was able to deliver the message word for word.

General Sumter was astonished that such a young woman had been brave enough to face danger and make such a long journey. He acted upon the message immediately and gathered his men. Within an hour, they made ready to march to the location specified by General Greene at British-held Orangeburg. Before leaving, however, he provided an armed escort for Emily's return journey home. He told the courageous girl, "South Carolina will never forget the debt of gratitude she owes to Emily Geiger."[57] His army arrived just in time. The two generals were able to force the British into retreat.

In 1900, the South Carolina Daughters of the American Revolution placed a marble memorial honoring Emily Geiger in the State Capitol at Columbia. It reads, "In memory of Emily Geiger's Ride, 1781."[58] When South Carolina created their state seal, they put a picture of Emily Geiger holding a laurel branch. There are also monuments in her honor at the Cayce Museum and South Carolina Statehouse.

10

Marquis de Lafayette—America's Friend

1777–1783	The War of Independence

Who Was the Marquis de Lafayette?

Though he came from a long line of **aristocrats**, Marie-Joseph Paul Yves Roch Gilbert du Motier de La Fayette (or Layfayette) had never been in battle himself, for he was only 17 years old. He had made up his mind to sail to America to help the colonists win their war for independence from England. The French king had forbidden him to make this journey and actually threatened to imprison him. His family didn't want him to carry out this wild plan. But the Marquis de Lafayette had made his decision and he would stand by it. He would soon be helping the American colonists in their struggle for freedom from British tyranny. The United States would forever call him their friend; were it not for him, there might never have been a United States of America.

aristocrats: Nobility

The Young Marquis

In the summer of 1775, Lafayette learned of the colonists' uprising in the faraway land of America. He was with his regiment in the frontier garrison of Metz in northeast France. The Duke of Gloucester, brother of the British King George III, was telling about the great George Washington and the "rebels" who followed him. Gloucester, unlike his brother, was actually **sympathetic** to the Americans. He expressed his belief that their cause was **just**.

Young Lafayette peppered him with questions, and before the evening ended he had determined to travel to America "to fight for the liberty of men whose land he had never seen, whose tongue he could not speak and whose very cause had been so recently unknown to him."[59] Speaking of that evening he later explained, "When I first heard of the colonists' quarrel, my heart was **enlisted** and I thought only of joining my colors to those of the revolutionaries."[60]

sympathetic: Feeling agreement with

just: Right

He was introduced to a brave, dependable German who had trained in the military service of the French and had become a brigadier general. His name was Baron de Kalb. During the French and Indian War, Baron de Kalb had been sent to the colonies to determine the attitude of the colonists toward the British. He traveled extensively throughout the colonies, growing in respect for their spirit of independence. Now that the colonies were involved in a war for freedom, he resolved to join them in their fight for liberty.

enlisted: Wanting to be a part of

Silas Deane was a member of the first Continental Congress assigned by a secret committee as a minister to France. He was sent to try to enlist aid for the American cause. While in France he met Marquis de Lafayette and Baron de Kalb. He promised them hope for a commission as general in the American army in exchange for their aid. Deane wrote a letter to the Continental Congress telling why he was offering such a high commission. He explained that Lafayette's high-ranking family would be opposed unless he could go as an officer. "Above all, his zeal for the liberty of our provinces, are such as have only been able to engage me to promise him the rank of major general."[61]

At the time, France was secretly sending arms, clothing, and equipment to the Americans. France and England had long been rivals. Since France's defeat in the French and Indian War, the French had sought for a way to **undermine** Britain's growing empire. Siding with the Americans would be such an opportunity, but the time was not quite right for France to risk war. America was small and hadn't yet proved she could be successful. So France decided to help secretly and see how things progressed. Lafayette would have to leave France **covertly** to escape notice by the British ambassador, who had issued an order prohibiting French officials from going to America.

undermine: Lessen the power of

covertly: In a secret way

Leaving for America

Couples married young at that time in France. The Marquis and his wife Adrienne, daughter of the Duke of d'Ayen, had married in April 1744, when he was but 16 and she 14. Adrienne supported her husband's love of liberty and desire to fight for the Americans, but her father did not understand. Lafayette was not able to persuade his father-in-law to assist him financially, so he bought a ship with his own funds that he named *La Victoire* (*The Victory*) on which he would sail to America. He wrote a note to his father-in-law and also one to his wife who was now expecting their second child, explaining his plan. He assured his wife of his love and his plan to return soon, asking her to write to him often. Silas Deane wrote to Congress about Lafayette's departure: it "has occasioned much conversation here and though the court pretends to know nothing of the matter, his conduct is highly extolled by the first people in France."[62]

Arrival to America

Lafayette spent the 54 days of the voyage brushing up on his English and military tactics. When they arrived, they anchored off a quiet

South Carolina beach, out of sight of Charleston Bay, where British warships were **blockading** the entrance to the harbor. The French Marquis knelt on the sand when he reached land, vowing, "I will conquer or perish with the Americans' cause."[63]

The 19-year-old Marquis would have to convince Congress of his loyalty. Lafayette, de Kalb, and a few French officers who were traveling with them found a group of men dredging for oysters who offered to take them to Major Benjamin Huger's house. Huger advised Lafayette and his fellow officers to make the journey to Charleston by land, which was 70 miles away, for their safety. He even furnished the men with three horses, so they took turns riding and walking through the woods and swampy land. Huger arranged for a pilot to steer their ship around the blockade. Lafayette's ship arrived in port in Charleston the day after he arrived by land. Leading citizens were delighted to see the goods he had brought from Europe. After selling his goods, he sent his ship back to France.

blockading: Blocking

Off to Congress

Lafayette and de Kalb purchased carriages and horses and set off for Philadelphia. The roads were rutted and rough, and travel was slow, hot, and full of trials. However, nothing dampened Lafayette's enthusiasm for his mission. He wrote to Adrienne, "The farther north I go, the more I love this country and its people."[64] It took them 32 days to make the 800-mile journey to present their letters of recommendation from Silas Deane. When they finally arrived, they were met by a rude Massachusetts congressman who informed them that Congress did not need any more French officers seeking high pay and commissions. Lafayette, still not deterred, appealed to Congress. "After the sacrifices I have made, I have the right to exact two favors: one is to serve at my own expense and the other is to begin to serve as a volunteer."[65]

Congress agreed to the major general's commission that Silas Deane had promised him, but the Marquis would receive no pay, as he had suggested. Lafayette requested to serve directly under General Washington. His request was granted. From his first meeting with Washington, Lafayette was in awe of the great commander. Washington liked Lafayette and appreciated his **zeal** from the start. That day a life long friendship was kindled between the 45-year-old commander and the 19-year-old French nobleman. Washington came to treat Lafayette as he would a son.

zeal: Patriotic enthusiasm

Meeting the Army

The next day Washington asked the Marquis to join him as he reviewed the Continental troops. What Lafayette saw that day was

11,000 soldiers, mostly ragged, some without shoes, in want of food. None had proper uniforms and all lacked polished military tactics. Washington apologized for the state of the troops to which Lafayette replied, " I am here, sir, to learn, and not to teach."[66] That answer pleased Washington. On August 20, 1777, Lafayette became an official member of General Washington's army.

Lafayette's First Test

Five days after his 20th birthday, Lafayette faced his first big test. Washington was caught off guard when the British crossed the Brandywine Creek at two points, formed a loop, and attacked from the rear, threatening to cut off the Americans. Lafayette perceived that the main assault would take place on the right flank and asked Washington for permission to join General John Sullivan's men on the right.

When the enemy troops were within 20 yards, the Americans lost heart and began to run. Lafayette, galloping back and forth, reared his horse in the air and tried to **halt** the flight, but the men were overwhelmed by the enemy's charge and retreated to the safety of

halt: Stop

the woods. It was then that Lafayette realized he'd been hit — a musket ball tore through the calf of his left leg. He had to stop to apply a bandage to the bleeding wound and barely escaped capture. Washington found Lafayette, weak from blood loss but still trying to organize troops to defend a bridge over Chester Creek. The Americans had suffered 1,000 casualties, double the amount the British had received. Washington's physician re-bandaged Lafayette's wound and sent him to Philadelphia where it could be properly cared for. Washington was heard telling the doctor, "Treat him as if he were my son."[67]

Back in Action

After his leg had healed, Lafayette volunteered to accompany Nathanael Greene on a secret mission to learn the strength of British troops around Philadelphia. Greene, having observed Lafayette's bravery at Brandywine, had taken a liking to him. He wrote his to wife, "He is one of the sweetest-tempered young gentlemen. He has left a young wife and a fine fortune … to come and engage in the cause of liberty — this is a noble enthusiasm."[68] Lafayette led 400 riflemen through the woods. They came upon a British outpost, attacked, and drove the enemy troops back to their camp. General Greene sent a glowing report to Washington of Lafayette's bravery and skill in handling the skirmish. "The Marquis is determined to be in the way of danger," he wrote.[69] Washington persuaded Congress to grant Lafayette command of a division, offering him whichever division he wanted. Thus Lafayette became the Continental Army's youngest general.

The Winter at Valley Forge

It was December 1777. Washington chose to move his troops to Valley Forge because it had a lot of timber which they could use to build winter quarters. Washington hoped to rebuild his bedraggled army. In just a few weeks, they had built more than 2,000 log huts. The huts provided some shelter, but food was scarce and clothing lacking. Lafayette shared the hardships with his men, ate the same rations, and used his own money at times to buy them shoes and warm clothing.

In a letter Lafayette wrote to his father-in-law, he urged him to use any influence he had at the French court to gain more aid for the Americans. He stated again his deep commitment to the cause of liberty and the belief that the colonists could win with the help of France. France had heard of his successes. Even his father-in-law was now praising his efforts. The French court was proud of him and many young Frenchmen envied his courage and zeal. On May 1, 1778, Silas Deane's

brother rode into camp at Valley Forge and announced that France had recognized the independence of the United States! Lafayette was overjoyed!

More Tasks to Accomplish

Lafayette proved indispensable to Washington in so many ways. He was given charge of a team of spies and ordered to move as close to Philadelphia as possible to learn the British plans. He **executed** his job faithfully. At another time, Washington put Lafayette in charge of 4,000 men with orders to annoy British General Clinton's army, to keep them in the location most beneficial to Washington. Lafayette also helped him achieve victory at the famous Battle of Monmouth. The fighting then shifted to the south, and Lafayette played a key role in many decisive battles.

executed: Accomplished

Lafayette felt if he could return to France, he could persuade the French government to support a French-American invasion. He requested leave from the American army. He had been gone from home for two years. On February 6, 1779, he returned to France and was welcomed as a hero. Adrienne was thrilled to see her husband again and to know he was safe. "God has preserved, in the midst of

tremendous dangers, the most lovable person in the world," she said through tears of joy.[70]

The French court welcomed Lafayette. He was surrounded by the king's ministers who asked him many questions, congratulating him on his successes. On Christmas Eve 1779, Adrienne gave birth to their third child, whom they named George Washington. Lafayette persisted for more than a year to get French aid. He urged the King to send a **massive** naval force to America. On March 5, 1780, Lafayette boarded a ship bound for America with orders to resume his command and to inform Washington that a large French fleet with thousands of troops would soon be on its way.

massive: Very large

The French Will Help

Washington was delighted. He stated that without French help there would have been little chance of winning the war. Early in 1781, Washington sent Lafayette with 1,200 men to help defend Virginia. Lord Charles Cornwallis was determined to capture Lafayette and carry him off to England in chains. "The boy cannot escape me. I shall now proceed to **dislodge** him from Richmond."[71] Against overwhelming odds, Lafayette managed to pull his troops out of Richmond and avoid the British by hiding in the woods, firing on them **sniper-fashion**, and disappearing back into the woods. Local militiamen joined Lafayette, and his forces picked up strength as reinforcements arrived daily.

dislodge: Remove from power

sniper-fashion: Shooting from a hiding place

Cornwallis chose Yorktown as a base from which he could more easily keep in communication by sea with British General Clinton in New York. He also figured if he needed reinforcements at any point, it would be faster to have them arrive by ship. This decision sealed his fate and led to the end of the war. Lafayette quietly built up **fortifications** while also establishing a ring of artillery positions around Yorktown, hoping to hem in Cornwallis by land. He informed Washington that if the French fleet showed up, the British army would be trapped. Washington finally received word that the French fleet was on the way — 29 warships carrying 3,000 troops had sailed from the French West Indies. He sent the good news to

fortifications: Defenses

Lafayette and ordered him to stand firm and do all in his power to prevent Cornwallis from escaping by land. He would himself head that way with a French-American land force. By the time Washington arrived, the land force numbered almost 20,000 men.

The Siege of Yorktown

On October 9, the siege began. The battle raged. The British still held two strong redoubts from which they were firing intense volleys on the French and Americans. It was decided to give the honor of destroying one of these redoubts to Lafayette. On October 14, Lafayette and his 400 infantrymen charged. Hand-to-hand combat began. The first redoubt fell to the Americans under Lafayette in ten minutes. On October 17, Cornwallis asked for a truce to discuss terms of surrender. On October 19, the 8,000 troops under Lord Cornwallis formally surrendered. Cornwallis was so **humiliated** at his loss that he pretended to be sick and did not attend the surrender. Yorktown was the last major battle of the War of Independence, and on September 3, 1783, the Treaty of Paris was officially signed, recognizing America as an independent nation.

humiliated: Embarrassed

After the War

Lafayette returned home where he and Adrienne bought a home of their own to raise their growing family. A portrait of Washington hung in their living room along with a framed copy of the Declaration of Independence. When Adrienne gave birth to their fourth child, a daughter, they named her Virginie in honor of George Washington's home state. In the summer of 1784, Washington invited Lafayette to come visit America as a guest of the new nation. His arrival was met with much fanfare, the roar of cannons, and people lining the streets to give him honor.

A county in Pennsylvania was named after Lafayette, the first of hundreds of American buildings and streets to bear his name. It was a tearful parting between Washington and his dearly loved "adopted son" as Lafayette again departed for France. Lafayette told Adrienne, "I work for their happiness. The welfare of America is intimately linked with the happiness of all mankind; she will become the respected and safe **asylum** of virtue, integrity, tolerance, equality, and a peaceful liberty."[72]

asylum: One offering shelter

A full-length portrait of the Marquis de Lafayette still hangs in the Capitol building in Washington, D.C. to give honor to America's friend. "And no one, save Washington himself, could be given greater credit for the triumph of the brave little nation than the young French nobleman who loved it as his own."[73]

Glossary

amends: Make up for wrongdoing.

Anglican: Church of England.

appealed: Made an earnest plea.

apprenticed: Trained.

aristocrats: Nobility.

arrogantly: Proudly.

asylum: One offering shelter.

barricades: Blockades.

bayonet: Blades on muskets.

bear arms: Carry guns.

benediction: Blessing at the end of a service.

blockading: Blocking.

Boston Common: Historic public park located in downtown Boston.

British General Braddock: Commander in Chief for the 13 colonies.

bunting: Heavy cloth used to make flags.

commending: Praising.

commerce: Buying and selling goods.

confiscate: Seize.

consent: Permission.

Continental money: Paper money issued by the Continental Congress during the war.

courier: Messenger.

covertly: In a secret way.

coward: Person afraid of danger.

deprivation: Lack of basic necessities.

desolate: Bleak.

detaining: Delaying.

determination: Strong decision to accomplish a goal.

dislodge: Remove from power.

dodging: Moving to avoid.

draperies: Curtains.

engraving: Cutting designs in silver to print on paper.

enlisted: Wanting to be a part of.

escort: Someone to accompany her.

executed: Accomplished.

expel: Dismiss.

fervently: Passionately.

fife: Military flute.

flank: Side.

forge: Furnace for shaping metal.

fortifications: Defenses.

Fort William Henry: A fort near Lake George in New York.

halt: Stop.

hardy: Accustomed to hardship.

helm: Head.

Hessian mercenaries: German soldiers paid to fight.

humiliated: Embarrassed.

indiscriminately: Randomly.

implemented: Put in place.

imposed: Forced.

inevitable: Sure to happen.

just: Right.

knapsacks: Backpacks.

Loyalists: Those loyal to Great Britain.

magnanimity: Charity.

massive: Very large.

mentored: Trained.

minutemen: Colonists ready to fight at a minute's notice.

motto: Rallying cry.

muffle: Make quieter.

muskets: Light guns with a long barrel.

Parliament: British ruling body.

peril: Danger.

perilous: Very dangerous.

pest house: House where sick people stayed until they got well or died.

pillage: Steal from and destroy.

plight: Difficult situation.

plundered: Robbed.

pondering: Thinking about.

quarantined: Kept at home to prevent the spread of germs.

rampage: Violent or excited behavior that is reckless or destructive.

recruit: Sign up for the army.

Redcoats: Nickname for British soldiers because of their red uniforms.

redoubt: Temporary fortification.

regiments: Companies of soldiers.

reinforcements: More volunteers.

reluctantly: Hesitatingly.

reprimanded: Rebuked.

retreat: Withdraw.

reverently: With respect.

rheumatism: Painful inflammation of joints.

scout: Person who gathers information.

sentries: Soldier guards.

sexton: Person who looks after a church:

skirmishers: Those who engage the enemy in light combat to delay their movement.

skirmishes: Unexpected, irregular fighting.

sniper-fashion: Shooting from a hiding place.

staunch: Firm.

stealthily: Cautiously so they wouldn't be seen.

stockpiling: Storing up.

submissive: Obedient.

surveyor: One who measures land.

sympathetic: Feeling agreement with.

tactical: Strategic.

tactics: Plans of action.

toast: Few words of remembrance.

Tories: American colonists who supported the British side.

traitors: Betrayers of one's country.

truce: Agreement to stop fighting.

tyranny: Cruel, oppressive rule.

undermine: Lessen the power of.

upholstery: Fabric-covered furniture.

usurpations: Abuses of power to control others.

virtues: Qualities.

volley: Many bullets shot at the same time.

zeal: Patriotic enthusiasm.

Corresponding Curriculum

The *What a Character! Series* can be used alongside other Master Books curriculum for reading practice or to dive deeper into topics that are of special interest to students.

This book in the series features heroes of the American War for Independence, whose stories would incorporate well for students in grades 6–8 accompanying history, language arts, vocabulary words and definitions, as well as geography studies and cultural insights. We have provided the list below to help match this book with related Master Books curriculum.

Chapter 1: Paul Revere — Rider for Liberty

America's Story Vol. 3 | *The Fight for Freedom*
America's Struggle to Become a Nation | *Language Lessons for a Living Education*

Chapter 2: John Peter Gabriel Muhlenberg — The Fighting Parson

America's Story Vol. 3 | *The Fight for Freedom*
America's Struggle to Become a Nation | *Language Lessons for a Living Education*

Chapter 3: Betsy Ross — America's Flag

America's Story Vol. 3 | *The Fight for Freedom*
America's Struggle to Become a Nation | *Language Lessons for a Living Education*

Chapter 4: John Stark — Hero of Bennington

America's Story Vol. 3 | *The Fight for Freedom*
America's Struggle to Become a Nation | *Language Lessons for a Living Education*

Chapter 5: Mad Anthony Wayne — The Midnight Attack

America's Story Vol. 3 — *The Fight for Freedom*

America's Struggle to Become a Nation — *Language Lessons for a Living Education*

Chapter 6: John Sevier — The Battle of Kings Mountain

America's Story Vol. 3 — *The Fight for Freedom*

America's Struggle to Become a Nation — *Language Lessons for a Living Education*

Chapter 7: Reverend James Caldwell — The Fighting Chaplain

America's Story Vol. 3 — *The Fight for Freedom*

America's Struggle to Become a Nation — *Language Lessons for a Living Education*

Chapter 8: Nathanael Greene — The Fighting Quaker

America's Story Vol. 3 — *The Fight for Freedom*

America's Struggle to Become a Nation — *Language Lessons for a Living Education*

Chapter 9: Emily Geiger — A Dangerous Ride

America's Story Vol. 3 — *The Fight for Freedom*

America's Struggle to Become a Nation — *Language Lessons for a Living Education*

Chapter 10: Marquis de Lafayette — America's Friend

America's Story Vol. 3 — *The Fight for Freedom*

America's Struggle to Become a Nation — *Language Lessons for a Living Education*

Endnotes

1. Roberta Edwards, *Who Was Paul Revere?* (New York: Penguin Random House, 2011), p. 61.
2. Dorothy Canfield Fisher, *Paul Revere and the Minutemen* (New York: Random House, 1950), p. 140.
3. William Mace, *Mace's Beginner's History* (New York: Rand, McNally, 1909), p. 175.
4. Ibid., p. 175.
5. J.T. Headley, *The Chaplains and Clergy of the Revolution* (Collingswood, NJ: C Scribner, 1864, excerpted by Christian Beacon, 1976), p. 36.
6. Ibid., p. 36.
7. Ibid., p. 36.
8. Edward W. Hocker, *The Fighting Parson of the American Revolution* (Harrisonburg, VA: Sprinkle Publications, 2016, reprinted; originally published by the author in Philadelphia, PA, 1936), p. 70.
9. Ibid., p. 120.
10. Ibid., p. 122.
11. Headley, *The Chaplains and Clergy of the Revolution*, p. 37.
12. Ibid., p. 37.
13. Judith St. George, *Betsy Ross, Patriot of Philadelphia* (New York: Henry Holt and Co., 1997), p. 12.
14. Peter and Connie Roop, *Betsy Ross* (New York: Scholastic, 2001), p. 58.
15. James Buckley Jr., *Who Was Betsy Ross?* (New York: Penguin Random House, 2014), p. 94.
16. Ben Z. Rose, *John Stark: Maverick General* (Lincoln, Massachusetts: Treeline Press, 2007), p. 51.
17. Karl Crannell, *John Stark: Live Free or Die* (Stockton, New Jersey: OTTN Publishing, 2007), p. 46.
18. Rose, *John Stark: Maverick General*, p. 121.
19. Ibid., p. 124.
20. Ibid., p. 124.
21. Crannell, *John Stark: Live Free or Die*, p. 69.
22. Ibid., p. 71.
23. John R. Spears, *Anthony Wayne* (New York: D Appleton and Co., 1903), p. 4–5.
24. Hazel Wilson, *The Story of Mad Anthony Wayne* (New York: Grosset and Dunlap, 1953), p. 98–99.
25. Bob Wells, *Mad Anthony Wayne* (New York: GP Putnam›s Sons, 1970), p. 83.
26. Spears, *Anthony Wayne*, p. 153.
27. Ibid., p. 155.
28. Wilson, *The Story of Mad Anthony Wayne*, p. 110.
29. Ibid., p. 111.
30. Spears, *Anthony Wayne*, p. 159.
31. Wilson, *The Story of Mad Anthony Wayne*, p. 179.
32. William H. Mace, *Mace's Beginners' History* (New York: Rand McNally, 1909), p. 213.
33. Blaisdell and Ball, *Hero Stories from American History* (Boston, Massachusetts: Ginn and Co., 1903), p. 92.
34. Ibid., p. 94–95.
35. Francis Marion Turner, *Life of General John Sevier* (Johnson City, TN: Overmountain Press, 1997; first published by Neale Publishing Co, 1910), p. 60.
36. J.T. Headley, *The Chaplains and Clergy of the Revolution* (New York: Charles Scribner, 1864, excerpted by Christian Beacon, Collingwood, NJ, 1976), p. 62.
37. Ibid., p. 62.
38. Craig MacDonald, *The Rebel Reverend: An American Revolution Hero* (San Bernadino, CA: Mule Kick Publication, 2015), p. 9.
39. Headley, *The Chaplains and Clergy of the Revolution*, p. 65.
40. MacDonald, *The Rebel Reverend: An American Revolution Hero*, p. 11.
41. Ibid., p. 11.

42. "Hannah Caldwell: *A Turning Point in the American Revolution*." 2023. County of Union. March 24, 2023. https://ucnj.org/parks-recreation/cultural-heritage-affairs/hannah-caldwell/.
43. Headley The Chaplains and Clergy of the Revolution, p. 11.
44. Ibid., p. 66.
45. MacDonald, *The Rebel Reverend: An American Revolution Hero*, p. 13.
46. Ibid., p. 13.
47. Ibid., p. 13.
48. Headley, *The Chaplains and Clergy of the Revolution*, p. 67.
49. Elswyth Thane, *The Fighting Quaker: Nathanael Greene* (New York: Hawthorn Books, 1972), p. 20.
50. "George Washington to Members of Congress, 15 March 1777," *The Writings of George Washington*, Vol. 7.
51. William Mace, *Mace's Beginners History* (New York: Rand and McNally Co, 1900), p. 186.
52. Thane, *The Fighting Quaker: Nathanael Greene*, p. 218.
53. Ibid., p. 219.
54. Ibid., p. 220.
55. Ibid., p. 229.
56. Ibid., p. 221.
57. Edith Patterson Meyer, *Petticoat Patriots of the American Revolution* (New York: The Vanguard Press, 1976), p. 213.
58. Ibid., p. 213.
59. Hodding Carter, *The Marquis de Lafayette: Bright Sword for Freedom* (New York: Random House, 1958), p. 14.
60. Russell Freedman, *Lafayette and the American Revolution* (New York: Holiday House, 2010), p. 14.
61. Ibid., p. 18.
62. Ibid., p. 26.
63. Carter, *The Marquis de Lafayette: Bright Sword for Freedom*, p. 21.
64. Ibid., p. 30.
65. Ibid., p. 32.
66. Ibid., p.34.
67. Freedman, *Lafayette and the American Revolution*, p. 36.
68. Ibid., p. 38.
69. Ibid., p. 38.
70. Ibid., p. 55.
71. Ibid., p. 61.
72. Ibid., p. 71.
73. Carter, *The Marquis de Lafayette: Bright Sword for Freedom*, p. 76.